Paris RER Handbook

Brian Patton

Capital Transport

AUTHOR'S NOTE

While the Paris urban Métro functions as a clearly defined and self-contained system, the city's suburban rail lines do not fall so neatly into one category. This book aims to deal in detail with the history, rolling stock and operation of those lines which make up the network of the Réseau Express Régional (RER) and in a rather briefer form with those aspects of other suburban lines within the Region of Ile-de-France which share common facilities with RER lines. It is correct to October 2000.

Even within the RER network, there are fundamental differences of approach which make it difficult to draw a neat distinction between its lines and those not included in the system. While lines A and B, with a considerable measure of RATP control, function as regional metros, the other three lines are basically suburban lines which have been extended into, and in the first two cases across the central area. Although marketed as RER, they are not within SNCF differentiated from other suburban lines and indeed one service, that from Versailles (CH) to Versailles (RG), is worked as line C of the RER for part of its length and part of the general network for the remainder! Much of the rolling stock is used in common with other lines and depot facilities are shared. There are no special signalling systems and no dedicated works stock. In short, the only way in which SNCF RER operations can be defined is that they are called RER lines! The reader should therefore be aware that what may seem a self-contained system on paper may function otherwise in practice.

The services covered in this book are:

RER lines A–E

SNCF Suburban Services

From Gare du Nord to Luzarches, Persan-Beaumont via Montsoult, Valmondois and
  Pontoise and from Saint-Ouen to Valmondois. Many trains are extended to Creil.

From Gare de l'Est to Crécy-la-Chapelle, Nanteuil, Crouy-sur-Ourcq, La Ferté
  Gaucher and Provins and the cross-country link from Bondy to Aulnay-sous-Bois

From Gare de Lyon to Montereau, Souppes and Boignville

From Gare d'Austerlitz to Angerville

From Gare Montparnasse to Gazeran, Houdan and Nantes-la-Jolie

From Gare Saint-Lazare to La Verrière, Versailles (RD), Saint-Nom-la-Bretèche,
  Bréval, Port Villez and Cars and from La Défense to Cergy le Haut.

In compiling this book, I am most grateful for the help of Brian Hardy, who has given invaluable assistance, in particular with regard to rolling stock, and who also made available his collection of photographs, without which it would not have been possible to provide sufficient illustrations. I am also grateful to David Haydock and Chris Wilson for assistance with photographs. In Paris M Denis Falguier, Head of Development for SNCF services in Ile-de-France, patiently answered my many questions during a long interview and I must also thank him and his staff for providing much additional information. His colleague, M Bernard Simonot, kindly conducted me around the new stations of line E and answered my many queries on that line. I am also grateful to M Serge Sempeur, formerly of RATP, and to Mme Christine Coquelard of the Agence Audio-visuelle of RATP and her colleagues for assistance with photographs.

First published 2001
ISBN 185414 230 5
Published by Capital Transport Publishing, 38 Long Elmes, Harrow Weald, Middlesex
Printed by CS Graphics, Singapore
© Brian Patton and Capital Transport Publishing 2001

The front cover and title page photographs are by David Haydock
The back cover photograph was supplied by the RATP

CONTENTS

THE PARIS AREA

It is not possible fully to understand railway development in the Paris area without first briefly looking at the general historical background.

Until 1860, the city of Paris comprised the area roughly within the present day lines 2 and 6 of the Métro. In that year it was extended to its present limit by Napoléon III and since then has not been further extended. From 1871 to 1920 this area was surrounded by a line of fortifications whose existence had important social and economic consequences for the inhabitants; the line of the fortifications can still be traced by the names of the various gates, such as Porte de la Chapelle. Until very recent times, there were no towns of any size in the area immediately outside the city boundaries, except for the royal town of Versailles. There was no French equivalent of the important market towns such as Croydon or Kingston which surrounded London. The city centre has always housed a comparatively large proportion of the local population and, despite a decline over the twentieth century, continues to do so. The result of all this is that the urban development of Paris and the surrounding area has taken a form quite different to that of London and in turn this has had an effect on the development of the rail network.

The city itself is divided into twenty 'arrondissements' which are both postal districts and important units of local government. The area immediately beyond formed for many years the Département of the Seine, but has since been divided into three départements of Seine-Saint-Denis, Hauts-de-Seine and Val-de-Marne. Further out are the four départements of Seine et Marne, Yvelines, Essonnes and Val d'Oise. Together the city and these départements form the Région of Ile-de-France and much responsibility for overall planning, including transport, rests with the Région. The inner and outer suburbs are sometimes known, rather poetically, as 'la banlieue de la petite couronne' and 'la banlieue de la grande couronne' respectively, phrases which do not meaningfully translate into English! Unpoetically they could be rendered as 'the inner and outer Greater Paris area'.

Until the middle of the nineteenth century, Paris remained an essentially mediaeval city in its layout and the deficiencies of this were shown up as the population began to increase towards and beyond the two million mark, to reach 2.8 million by 1900. Under Baron Haussman, Préfet (Prefect) of the Seine under Napoléon III a great deal was achieved in modernising the city, with new streets and parks and an adequate system of sewage. However, he showed no interest in the suburbs. These policies were continued under Marshal Mac Mahon, second president of the Third Republic, by Adolphe Alphand, Director of Roads, Public Works and Architecture for Paris. Alphand showed considerable interest in transport, although he tended to favour an urban rail network and was generally hostile to the main line railway companies. He was also commissioner-general for the very successful universal exhibition of 1889. Under his direction, many slums were cleared and replaced by housing of a higher standard, at higher rents. There was also considerable industrial development within the city, but, by 1880, pressure on space and also on rents began to displace some of this activity to the suburbs, along with some of the working population. This movement created a demand for cheap travel for these workers and, under pressure from David Raynal, Minister for Public Works in the early 1880s, the main line companies agreed to introduce cheap returns and weekly tickets for workmen, available on designated trains only. These came into operation in 1884/5. In the former year, the number of journeys made on these tickets was 940,494, a figure which had increased to almost six million ten years later, and had doubled again by 1900, in which year there were about 100,000 daily commuters from the suburbs into city. The age of suburban travel had truly begun. There was also a certain amount of outward commuting and, as in Scottish cities, a fair number of workers went home for lunch, creating a lesser, but still important, midday peak. Sunday brought heavy pleasure traffic.

The movement to the suburbs increased markedly after the First World War. Although all rail lines serving Paris were affected, it was those of the État which carried by far the largest percentage from Saint-Lazare, Invalides and Montparnasse, but especially the first of these. The annual number of passengers on the suburban lines of this railway increased from 69 million in 1913 to 85 million in 1921 and, despite a setback during the time of economic crisis in 1931, had still reached 126.6 million in 1936. The deficit on these workings increased more than correspondingly, from 10 million francs in 1913 to 122 million in 1936. While all companies showed comparable trends, none approached the global figures of the État; the total number of suburban passengers in 1936 was 272 million, the balance of 150 million being divided among the other four companies, although not in equal proportion.

After the upheaval of the Second World War, the movement to the suburbs continued at an increased rate and the number of suburban passengers reached 316 million in 1959 and 404 million in 1972; the total carried in 1998 was 527.8 million. The generally unplanned development of the suburban area until the late 1950s brought some social problems in its wake, quite apart from the problems for SNCF, and in 1965 the government of the Fifth Republic published the first Schéma Directeur d'Aménagement et Urbanisme de la Région Parisienne for the Paris region. This included transport planning and led to the development of what today is known as the RER. The most recent trend has been that of a considerable growth of inter-suburban commuting and a slight decline in the numbers of people living in the suburbs and commuting daily to the central area of Paris, which has remained at just over one million since 1975.

In the early years of the RER as an identifiable network, middle-day off-peak services were operated by three-car trains, as shown by a three-car set in original livery arriving at Fontenay-sous-Bois. Now three-car trains of MS stock are confined to late evening workings. *Brian Hardy*

THE ADMINISTRATIVE STRUCTURE

Railways in France were, as in Britain, generally operated by private companies, but some were constructed by the state and in all cases there was very much more central planning and control of the building of new lines than was the case in Britain. In most cases this was done by the granting of concessions and in general there was little duplication of lines between Paris and other towns and cities. While this avoided much wasteful competition, it did also mean that there was less chance of spreading heavy traffic between the lines of different companies.

After early amalgamations, there were six major companies operating French railways, all but one of these serving Paris. These five were the Chemin de Fer du Nord (Northern Railway), Chemins de Fer de l'Est (Eastern Railways), Chemins de Fer de l'Ouest (Western Railways), Chemin de Fer Paris–Orléans (Paris–Orléans Railway, PO) and Chemin de Fer Paris–Lyon–Méditerranée (Paris, Lyon and Mediterranean Railway, PLM). The Ouest was in more or less constant financial difficulties (due in no small measure to its suburban traffic) and in 1908 it was taken over by the state, being thereafter known as the Chemins de Fer de l'État (State Railways). On 1 January 1938 the railways were nationalised as the Société Nationale des Chemins de Fer Francais (French National Railways).

The Paris termini of these railways were all situated at some distance from the centre of the city and much of the railway history of the nineteenth century is a record of attempts by the private companies to obtain permission to bring their lines further into Paris. In this they came up against opposition from the City Council, which was more interested in developing a local network, but two companies, the PO and the Ouest, did succeed in their goal in 1900, which was a significant year in the history of transport in Paris.

After 1919, when suburban operation was no longer perceived as a source of profit, this interest in extending into the city centre waned and the way was clear for co-operation with the local authorities and the urban network.

However, the first active step towards co-operation was not taken until the Law of 21 March 1948 set up the Régie Autonome des Transports Parisiens (RATP) to operate bus (and later also tram) services and the urban Métro, and the Office Régional des Transports Parisiens (ORTP) to co-ordinate all services, including those of SNCF, fix fares and draw up plans for the future. In practice, the last of these did not result in much action on the ground (or under it!) and the 1950s were a period of stagnation for the suburban network. The RATP was expected both to provide a public service and balance its budget, but no increase in fares was allowed by the ORTP (under pressure from all the ever-changing governments of the Fourth Republic) between August 1951 and February 1958. As a result its deficit had reached 16.4 milliard (old) francs by 1957 (roughly £16.4 million at contemporary rates of exchange). It was clear that this state of affairs could not continue and by a decree of 7 January 1959, the government of the new Fifth Republic replaced the ORTP by the Syndicat des Transports Parisiens (STP), which has much wider powers over investment.

As in Britain, the nationalised railways continued for many years to be organised as regions but in 1970 SNCF created a special section of management for the railways of the Paris area, to work closely with RATP, central government and the local authorities. Until very recently this section was based in the former Ouest/État offices at 88, rue Saint-Lazare but it has now been transferred to Montparnasse. This section developed a programme of major works for the suburban network, to be funded in part by the state (30%) and by the local authorities (30%). With finance of this nature assured, it is not surprising that it was possible to launch a programme of new construction which would be the envy of less fortunate cities. For the purpose of this operation, the extent of the designated suburban network was enlarged to reach a route length of 986km.

By a decree of 1 January 1991, the area of competence of the STP was greatly enlarged to be co-terminous with the boundaries of Ile-de-France Region. The area of operation of the Carte Orange (q.v.) was adjusted at the same time and the former SNCF department of Paris suburban services became the Direction d'Ile-de-France. The area now covered serves a population of 10.6 million inhabitants, with 374 stations and 1,275 route kilometres. This alteration did have the effect of bringing back into local control some diesel worked services, the previous area having reached 100% electrification in 1988. The stable financial regime and the close integration of local planning and transport have now given this Region a network of efficient services which other less developed countries can only envy.

The most recent development has been a re-branding of the suburban network. As the term 'banlieue' has acquired negative connotations over recent years – many passengers associate it with anti-social behaviour on trains and insecurity – the network has in 2000 been relaunched as 'Transilien SNCF'. This term is a compound of 'transport' and 'Francilien', the name of an inhabitant of Ile-de-France. The regional colours have given way to blue with green relief, this being in the form of a leaf, to emphasise the green credentials of the network. To date the new scheme has been applied only to some units of class Z6400 and it remains to be seen how it will look on double-deck stock.

Apart from the renovation of class Z6400 and the delivery of new stock, it is intended that the new brand name will be a mark of quality. Associated with this will be an increased staff presence on stations and installation of video cameras, to give increased personal security. Stations will be renovated and signage for interchange will be improved – it is intended to carry out this programme on 250 stations in the next three years. During this period also, the Infogare system will be extended to cover 70% of all stations and, with the back up of additional staff, will provide real-time information in the event of any irregularity in the service. Trains running beyond zone 5 will, after 21.00, carry on-board staff to assist passengers and reinforce security.

The new Transilien logo and colour scheme have now been applied to most SNCF RER stations, as seen at Chaville-Vélizy in July 2000.
Brian Patton

THE EVOLUTION OF THE RER NETWORK

LINE A

THE WESTERN NETWORK

The first railway in the Paris area and the third in France was the line from Paris to Saint-Germain, built by the financiers Emile and Isaac Pereire and opened to Le Pecq on 24 August 1837 by Queen Marie-Amélie, the ministers of King Louis-Philippe having persuaded him not to chance his luck on so risky a venture. Public service began two days later. The line started from a station at the Place de l'Europe, passed under the Batignolles hill by a tunnel and, having twice crossed the Seine, terminated at Le Pecq, further progress towards Saint-Germain being barred by a steep hill, beyond the power of contemporary locomotives. The Paris terminus was intended to be only temporary and the Pereires had already acquired property to permit an extension inwards to Madeleine. This was, however, rejected on environmental grounds. The line proved to be very popular, particularly with excursionists, although with fares ranging from one franc to 1.60 francs, when an average workman's wage was two francs per day, it attracted a mainly middle- and upper-class clientele.

The final 1.5km section to Saint-Germain was completed in 1847 and opened on 14 April of that year. This part of the line was worked by atmospheric power and the ruling gradient of 35mm/m necessitated some heavy engineering works. These included a cutting across the park surrounding the château, which completely ruined the classical symmetry of the gardens laid out by Le Nôtre, but nobody seemed to mind at the time. The system worked well enough for twelve years, though it was liable to interruption in wet weather, when water entered the pipe, but when more powerful steam locomotives became available, it was converted to conventional operation in 1859. From then until electrification, a banking engine was attached to all outbound trains at Le Pecq.

Further lines were soon added to the original one and by 1855 the western suburban network had reached Versailles Rive-Droite (RD) (2 August 1839), Mantes, on the main line to Rouen (9 May 1843), Argenteuil (28 April 1851) and Auteuil (2 May 1854). The addition of the Versailles service placed a considerable strain on the facilities of the original terminus and it was replaced by the first Gare Saint-Lazare in 1843. Fortunately the brothers Pereire had taken the precaution of buying up much of the surrounding land and there was plenty of room for expansion at a later date. Between 1886 and 1889 the entire complex was rebuilt into its present form to a design of the Ouest's architect, Justin Litsch. When the City turned down his plans for a grand square in front of the station, he hid a considerable part of the new façade with the Hôtel Terminus (now Concorde – Saint-Lazare) and in consequence it is difficult to appreciate the vast extent of the station from outside. Since then it has remained, it terms of train movements, the busiest terminus in Paris, due largely to its suburban traffic.

The various individual companies using Saint-Lazare did not always live together harmoniously and it was recognised that, in the long term, amalgamation would be beneficial to all of them. In 1855 they came togayher with the original Chemin de Fer de l'Ouest, which had opened the line from Montparnasse to Versailles Rive-Gauche (RG) on 10 September 1840. These now formed the Chemins de Fer du Nord-Ouest. The 'Nord' was soon dropped from the title and this company was known as the Ouest. It went on to become the French equivalent of the Great Eastern Railway in England and much of its later history is a record of its attempts to keep abreast of its suburban traffic. This grew steadily throughout the century but particularly after the introduction of workmen's returns, at 50% more than the single third class fare, on 17 July 1883. Weekly tickets were introduced in the following year. As a result of these measures, suburban traffic at Saint-Lazare had reached 26 million passengers per annum by 1888. The measures adopted to cope with this increase included the opening of a relief line for Saint-Germain trains (1892) and the institution of separate 'omnibus' services for the inner area with 'semi-directs' serving the outer area (1893).

The Ouest also developed the double-deck concept for suburban carriages. There had already been some primitive vehicles of this type, based on stage coach design, on the Saint-Germain line but the first purpose-built double-deck coaches were placed in service in 1853, by the first Ouest company. These were two-axle vehicles, with four second class compartments in the lower deck, seating 40, and space for 24 third class passengers in three bays on the upper deck, which was roofed but open at the sides. It was reached by a straight stairway at each end of the carriage, leading to a walkway only 42cm wide around the upper deck, this being entirely unprotected by handrails. Headroom on this deck, at 1.37m, was extremely limited and there was no kind of lighting. A slightly larger version, still with open sides on the upper deck, was built by the new Ouest in 1855 and there were further developments of the design in 1864 and 1879. The final coaches of the type were delivered in 1894 and had four and a half seating bays on top. The Est, Nord and Petite Ceinture paid the Ouest the compliment of copying the design in large numbers. By the end of the century, the Ouest had almost 600 such coaches on its books. However, there were accidents, particularly among returning excursionists on Sunday evenings, and in 1898 the government began to agitate for the removal of the type from service. But while they were successful with the other operators, there were just too many of the design in service with the Ouest and they had to admit defeat. The last did not disappear from service until 1931 – and even then some were sold off for further service in Egypt!

From 1895 an enclosed double-deck design was developed, based on coaches already used on the Est. These coaches were still two-axle vehicles, but had a lower floor level and were built to more generous dimensions. The upper deck was totally enclosed and consisted of five seating bays, reached by a central corridor. Headroom, at 1.7m, was improved, but was still a problem for anyone of above average height. At last passengers on this deck could enjoy the luxury of lighting, there being two oil lamps per saloon; these were later replaced by gas lamps and later still by electricity. These double-deckers were nicknamed 'Bidels' by Parisians, who thought that the commuters crowded into the spartan vehicles, which had bars along the windows of the upper deck, bore more than a passing resemblance to the monkeys in the cages of M Bidel's travelling menagerie. Normally they were worked as trains of 24 coaches, with a seating capacity of 1,932, plus as many standees as could cram aboard. Identical coaches were built by the Est and the last of that company's fleet was withdrawn as late as 1953. An example of each type of double-decker is preserved in the railway museum in Mulhouse, the 'Bidel' being one built for the Est.

As early as 1849, the Saint-Germain company had found it inconvenient to work suburban trains with tender engines and in that year had rebuilt one of these into a 2–2–2 tank. It went on to develop a 2–4–0 tank design and later an 0–6–0 of very British appearance. The last new tank type to appear before electrification was a handsome 2–6–2 design in 1910. All these types worked on the Saint-Germain line at different times.

Despite the 'Bidels' and the other improvements, the suburban network and in particular the Saint-Germain line were rapidly approaching saturation, with Saint-Lazare handling in 1890 385 trains per day, of which 46 were for that line. It is not surprising that the Ouest showed early enthusiasm for electrification and in that same year made trials of a Heilmann steam-electric locomotive, named 'La Fusee' (The Rocket). Further trials in the area of Le Havre in the following year showed that, while the concept was technically successful, such engines were unlikely to be capable of moving a loaded suburban train and attention turned to all-electric power. Between 1895 and 1900 trials were conducted between Saint-Germain and Saint Germain GC with two two-axle locomotives, each built on one bogie of 'La Fusee'. Both third rail and overhead current collection were tested, although the latter soon had to be abandoned due to problems of isolation of current with steam locomotives running under the wires. Conducted under the direction of Natalis Mazen, the company's electrical engineer, the trials were deemed to be a success, but unfortunately they had no immediate outcome as far as the Saint-Germain line was concerned.

However, in 1913 the railway, by now the État, published a plan devised by Mazen in 1907, for the electrification of the suburban network. The principles behind the scheme had much in common with those of today's RER – separation of suburban from main line traffic, the use of high platforms at stations, reversibility of train sets fitted with automatic couplers and the employment of all-metal rolling stock of a high degree of reliability. The plan also envisaged the construction of a new underground station at Saint-Lazare and the opening out of the Batignolles tunnels. Third rail current collection, at 600V DC, would be employed.

War prevented immediate implementation of these plans but studies were resumed in 1920 and were given added impetus by the explosive growth of suburban traffic which began after the war. In 1913 the suburban services of the État had handled just under 70 million passengers, whereas by 1924 this figure had reached over 95 million and was still climbing. An explosion of a rather more fatal kind also played a part in the alterations. In the evening rush hour of 5 October 1921, two departing trains collided in the Batignolles tunnel and the debris caught fire, this in turn igniting the gas cylinders, which exploded with devastating force. Twenty-eight people were killed and thirty seriously injured and only swift action by staff on the spot averted a worse tragedy. The railway companies were immediately ordered by the government to remove gas lighting from all trains and the État complied by fitting suburban trains with generator vans.

The tunnel was replaced by a cutting and it was found possible to install two additional tracks. Electrification began in 1924 and reached Saint-Germain on 20 March 1927. By comparison with steam operation, there was a saving of 18 minutes on the journey. With electrification and the adoption of automatic block signalling, it was found possible to accommodate all trains within the existing station and the idea of an underground terminal was abandoned.

With the towers of La Défense in the background, Standard stock motor coach 545 awaits departure for Issy-Plaine at Puteaux on 13 October 1980. This particular coach, a driving trailer, was one of a small batch of ten built by Deschouches-David et Cie in 1929. This line now forms part of tram line T2 and the terminus (at La Défense) is underground. *Brian Patton*

The motor-driving trailer sets which served the electrified lines were built for reliability and strength rather than for comfort and speed. They had four 165hp motors and either electro-magnetic or electro-pneumatic control. There were ultimately 205 sets, all more or less identical in design, despite having been supplied by six different manufacturers, in four separate batches, normally referred to as the third, fourth, fifth and sixth series. Collectively they were known as 'Standard' stock. The only significant variation was in 40 motor coaches which had a driving cab at each end to permit solo operation on the Auteuil line in off peak periods. The all-metal coaches weighed 57 tonnes for motor coaches and 39 tonnes for trailers and in service they had none of the sparkle of the Southern Electric or the Berlin S-Bahn. However, they were supremely reliable and some sets ran 3.5 million kilometres during their lifetime. On the Saint-

Coach 5681 is at the rear of an outbound train of Z5600 stock on line C approaching Chaville-Vélizy on line C on 22 July 2000. *Brian Patton*

Germain line, an emergency procedure had been devised to cope with a breakdown on the gradient leading from Le Pecq to the terminus, but during the period of operation of the Standard stock, it was not once necessary to implement this.

The Standard stock did not change much during its lifetime. The white roofs of the Etat livery gave way to a drab all-over green in SNCF days, when the stock was numbered Z1300 to Z1500. The line voltage was increased to 700V in 1931 and to 750V after 1960, but this had no visible effect on the trains. The stock was gradually withdrawn as lines were converted to 25kV AC in the 1970s and the last set ran on the Auteuil line (*q.v.*) on 6 January 1985. One set has been set aside for preservation in the railway museum.

After electrification traffic continued to increase and at the formation of SNCF the Saint-Germain line was carrying 40 million passengers per year, with twenty eight-coach trains at peak times, each train being capable of carrying 1,300 passengers. After a brief decline in the early 1950s, the upward trend was resumed and by 1960 it was clear that Saint-Lazare, with almost a quarter of a million passengers per day, had once again reached saturation and that only by removing one service would relief be obtained. The Saint-Germain line was clearly the most likely candidate.

Outward bound to Chessy, a unit of class M184 leaves the tunnel of line A at Saint-Mandé in July 2000. The abandoned formation and the closed tunnel of the original line to Bastille can be seen in the centre of the photograph. *Brian Patton*

THE EASTERN NETWORK

By comparison with the western suburbs, the eastern quarters of Paris were largely neglected by the early railway entrepreneurs. It was the development of the Bois de Vincennes as a public park by Napoléon III which gave rise to the first concrete plans for lines in this area. The government considered a plan devised by Arnoux and based on the Sceaux line (*q.v.*) for two lines, but rejected this in favour of a plan put forward by the Chemin de Fer de Strasbourg (the future Est company) for a line from Place de Bastille to La Varenne. There were some problems over the Paris terminus and ultimately the company obtained its chosen site only as a result of arbitration by the Emperor himself. Construction began in 1855 and the line was opened without any ceremony on 22 September 1859.

The station at Bastille, designed by the architect Berthelin, was of modest dimensions and right up to the end of operation it was necessary to use a traverser if the locomotive had to be released from an incoming train. The first kilometre of line from the terminus ran on a viaduct about 9m above the level of the Avenue Daumesnil. A connexion with the Petite Ceinture was made at Bel-Air and the total length of the line was 16.81km.

Possibly because of its extremely cheap fares and a regular interval service, the Vincennes line, as it became known, was an instant success, with a good balance of regular and excursion traffic. As specified in its original contract, the line also provided one workmen's train per day. In 1869 almost six million passengers were carried. Expansion was temporarily held back by the extensive damage inflicted on the line during the Franco-Prussian war and the civil strife of the Commune which followed, but once matters had settled down again, it was extended in three stages to Brie-Comte-Robert, reached on 5 August 1875. A connexion with the Grande Ceinture was established in 1877 and trains on that line used the tracks of the Vincennes line between Champigny and Sucy-Boneuil. Further extension to Verneuil l'Etang, where a link was made to the main line, followed on 1 July 1892, but this section, which was built primarily for strategic reasons, traversed an area which was and remained rural and brought much less profit to the Est. The total length of line was now 54.1km. By 1900 19 million passengers were being carried per year, but from that year competition from the newly electrifed tramways of the Chemins de Fer Nogentais and the Métro made life more difficult. Electrification was considered but rejected and instead the Est bought some powerful steam tank locomotives of class 32000 (later SNCF class 131TB) and instituted a 15-minute headway and also some semi-direct trains which served only the more important stations.

Double-deck carriages of the Ouest design, but with curved stairs, were used from 1859 to 1900 and enclosed 'Bidels' first appeared in 1884 and lasted until 1953, by which time they were the last of the type in service.

Just before the outbreak of war in 1939, the line was cut back to Boissy-Saint-Léger, but it remained intact and in 1943 a limited service was restored to Brie. It was also used as a diversionary route for main line trains which were unable to reach Gare de l'Est during the period 1944–46.

Thereafter the line reverted to purely suburban operation, gradually acquiring its own very individual character. Those who operated it gained the nickname of 'Bastillards' (Bastille men). Ex-German coaches handed over as war reparations were used from 1948 but were in turn replaced by push-pull stock

Class 141TB450 (2–8–2) awaits departure from the former Bastille terminus with a train for Boissy-Saint-Léger in April 1968. The locomotive is one of a large series built for the Est before and during the first world war. The train is made up of ex-Est all-metal push-pull stock of the 1930s; the third class vehicles had three doors per side, instead of the more usual two. In accordance with normal SNCF practice with such trains, the locomotive is at the "country" end. *Brian Patton*

of Est design. More powerful locomotives of type 141TB took over in the 1950s. In 1953 service was again cut back to Boissy and the line beyond was singled. Apart from the replacement of some level crossings by bridges, the Vincennes line then suffered a period of planning blight while discussion went on about the regional system and in the 1960s it looked distinctly run-down. There were then 44 trains each way per day. Nevertheless many of those who worked on it, and some regular passengers, regretted when the last train left Bastille in the small hours of 14 December 1969, to be replaced by the shining new trains of the RER on the following day.

THE SCEAUX LINE

In the 1830s the village of Sceaux, lying directly to the south of Paris, numbered only 1,670 inhabitants, though on Sundays and holidays it was a favourite
pleasure resort for people from the city, most of whom travelled there in a kind
of horse carriage known as a 'coucou' (cuckoo). Nonetheless the local people had
shown interest in the construction of a railway which would link the village to
the city. After much lobbying, they obtained a concession – but a concession for
no ordinary railway.

Jean-Claud Republicain Arnoux had served as a lieutenant in the armies of
Napoléon I and on the return of peace found himself unemployed. He went to
work in road transport and then began to study the building of the first railway lines. He noted that these required heavy earthworks, with considerable
associated expense, to provide a line which was within the capabilities of contemporary locomotives. He also realised that no research had been undertaken
into alternatives to the rigid two-axle wheelbase for carriages or to the chain
couplings, which were a source of discomfort to passengers and a danger in accidents. In 1838 he published a pamphlet 'Système de Voitures pour Chemins de
Fer de toute Courbure' (Rolling Stock for Railways of any Curvature) and then
patented his ideas.

In some respects Arnoux's ideas, which were derived from a study of the
dynamics of road vehicles, are strikingly modern and certain aspects of them
can be seen in practice on present-day light rail vehicles. Briefly, he devised a
system of articulated trains with pivoted axles, in which the first axle of the
leading carriage was steered by two forks which touched the track; it commu-
nicated any change of direction to the next axle by two crossed chains. In turn,
this was connected to the first axle of the next carriage by a fixed coupling and
any change of direction was conveyed by this. In this manner, the axles felt any
change of direction a few seconds before they actually entered a curve, with a
consequent reduction in the transmission of jolts to the coach body. The wheels
were mounted independently on the axles to allow for rotation at different
speeds. Finally the gauge was to be as wide as possible, to increase the steadi-
ness of the ride. Arnoux claimed that his system would allow railways to be built
at low cost in difficult terrain, providing a service to the public in places which
would otherwise be out of reach of the growing network. Having tested his ideas
first in model form then on two circular lines at Saint-Mandé, Arnoux then
indicated his willingness to operate a new line without any subsidy. To the
government, wondering how to satisfy the inhabitants of Sceaux, this seemed a
heaven-sent opportunity and accordingly Arnoux was given the concession for
the new line. This received royal assent on 6 September 1844 and was to run
for fifty years.

Unfortunately there were two provisions which were to militate against the
profitable operation of the line. The city terminus was to be located at the
Barrière de l'Enfer, very near the present station of Denfert-Rochereau and even
now a considerable distance from the city centre. In 1844 this location was
almost in the country. Moreover to test the claims that the system could operate in difficult terrain, the course of the line between Bourg-la-Reine and Sceaux
was laid out almost as that of a mountain railway, with a ruling gradient of
11.5%, instead of following the direct and much easier route. The gauge was to

be 1.751m. Both termini were laid out as loops and points allowed trains to enter from either direction, depending on the wind, so that passengers waiting on the single platform would not be inconvenienced by smoke and smuts from the locomotive.

Construction began in 1845 and, despite very wet weather, pressed ahead sufficiently rapidly to allow opening of the line on 23 June 1846. (Other sources give the date as 7 June.) It was an instant success, especially on Sundays, when would-be passengers had sometimes to be turned away. It was therefore decided to double part of the line and obtain additional locomotives for 1847 and to allow for this expenditure, additional shares were issued. These were not taken up in full and the financial situation of the line deteriorated rapidly to such an extent that it passed into receivership in December 1848 and was for the next two years worked by the state. In those circumstances, the concession for an extension from Bourg-la-Reine to Orsay, obtained in 1846, could not be used. The troubles arose from the original under-capitalisation of the company and were in no way connected with the Arnoux system, which was proving technically very satisfactory.

The station building at Denfert Rochreau still shows clearly its original semi-circular façade. This view was taken in November 1996. *Brian Patton*

The high level platforms also still show traces of the original layout. Motor coach Z23335 is stabled in one of the sidings. *Brian Hardy*

Back again in private ownership from 1 November 1850, the line began to experience a modest improvement in its fortunes and work could be started on the extension to Orsay, which was opened on 29 July 1854. But despite increasing traffic, the financial situation remained precarious and it was unable to buy enough new rolling stock to take advantage of all the traffic offered by this extension. However, just when matters seemed to be at their worst, the line suddenly became of interest to the Paris Orléans company, whose fortunes were being threatened by proposals made by the Grand Central Railway and its associated companies to gain access to Paris. Talks were begun in great secrecy and on 18 June 1857 the Sceaux line became part of the main line network.

On 26 August 1867 an extension was opened from Orsay to Limours, still using the Arnoux system and some new and more powerful locomotives and new rolling stock. Traffic was seriously interrupted by the Franco-Prussian war of 1870–71 and normal service was not resumed until July 1871. Thereafter the line settled down to twenty years of reliable and reasonably profitable service. But with the growth of the national network, its non-standard features became more and more of a problem, especially on the freight side. The Grande Ceinture had reached Massy-Palaiseau in 1883 but through working was of course impossible. In that year, the grant of further concessions to the PO company was made conditional on the conversion of the Sceaux line to standard gauge. The main line to Limours was duly converted in May 1891. By dint of very careful planning, this was done overnight, on the night of 21/22 May. The Sceaux branch followed in May 1893 but in this case, conversion was not simply a matter of substituting standard gauge track for the broad gauge; many sharp curves had to be eased and the steep and tortuous approach to Sceaux was abandoned in favour of the direct line still used today.

Thus ended an interesting experiment, technically successful, but needing careful maintenance, and capable of development had there existed the political will for this. The tight curves which still exist on the line in the inner suburbs bear witness to its unusual conception.

At the same time as the conversion was being planned, the PO began to consider an inward extension of the line to bring it nearer to the centre of Paris. Ideally it would have liked to join the line on to its main line in the area of Gare d'Austerlitz, but any such junction was ruled out by the municipal authorities and the extension ended at Gare de Luxembourg. Authorisation was given in January 1892 and work on the 2.16km extension began immediately. It ran in tunnel for most of its length and the terminal sidings at Luxembourg were laid out in such a way as to permit a future extension northwards. The extension opened for traffic on 1 April 1895. The company had hoped for a presidential inauguration, but President Faure was ill and they had to make do with the Minister for Public Works, M Dupoy-Dutemps, who performed a ceremonial opening on 31 March. As the terminus was completely underground, there could have been a considerable problem of ventilation, even though the 0–6–0 tank locomotives were fitted with condensing apparatus and burned coke. To reduce the nuisance, a large extractor fan was installed in the basement of the property which included the station entrance and this was connected by a series of tunnels to the platform area. Fresh air was drawn into this system by a series of grilles in the pavement of the street above, concealed in decorative kiosks, and it was claimed that the air in the station was completely changed every 24 minutes. Operation in the tunnel section was controlled by an early form of colour light signalling, which provided a single white light for clear and two red

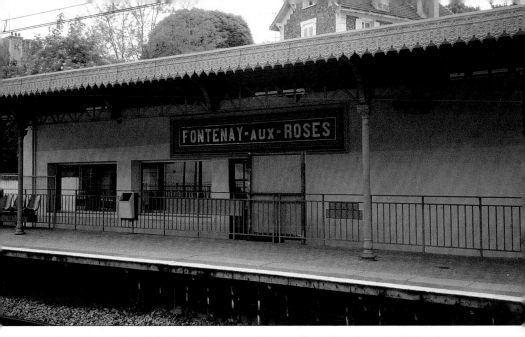

A view of the northbound platform at Fontenay-aux-Roses on line B. Note the ornate tiled station name and the ornate edge to the platform canopy. *Brian Hardy*

and one white light for danger. High level platforms were provided at the stations on the extension and the loop at Denfert-Rochereau was disconnected, although terminal platforms at the upper level at this station continued to be used by extra trains to Limours.

The line then settled down to another period of tranquility, with a steady increase in passenger numbers from just under two million in 1895 to just under twelve million in 1914. Commuters began to outnumber those pleasure-seekers who were lured by the PO posters to use the line to reach the waterfalls at Vaux de Cernay (by cab from Boullay-les-Troux) or to enjoy the sedate pleasure of donkey rides at Sceaux. To cope with this growth, the company ordered new 2–8–2 tank locomotives to replace the little 0–6–0s, but due to the outbreak of war, these did not arrive until 1920.

The new motive power came just in time. The 1920s saw a spectacular growth of low-cost housing in the suburbs as developers (often of an unscrupulous nature) bought up large tracts of countryside and sold these off as lots for housing, generally without providing the basic infrastructure. About 200,000 families or roughly 700,000 people then moved out of the central area to occupy what were often narrow, jerry-built houses, which they bought through building societies. On the Sceaux line, the countryside out as far as Bourg-la-Reine disappeared under streets of such housing and this led to an increase in traffic to 15 million passengers by 1930. The junction with the Grande Ceinture was rebuilt and many level crossings were replaced by bridges, but there was no attempt to modernise the rolling stock and the two-axle coaches bought in 1895 continued to bump their way in and out of Luxembourg. Passengers began to vote with their feet, to the greater profit of the buses of the STCRP, and by 1937 the number of passengers had fallen to eight million. Closure or total modernisation were the only answers.

The possibility of electrifying the line had been considered before 1914 but serious discussion did not begin until 1929, between the PO company and the Ministry of Public Works. It was proposed that the line as far as Sceaux and Massy-Palaiseau should be transferred to the ownership of the Département of the Seine and electrified. The matter was held up while a public enquiry was held to consider the position of the Département of Seine-et-Oise, which had protested at its exclusion from the scheme, but this upheld the original concept. Agreements were then made between the PO and the CMP in 1931, under which the former was to electrify the Sceaux line, the costs being met by the Département of the Seine, while the latter was to operate it. By the Law of 10 April 1932 the line was officially re-classified as being 'd'interêt local', losing its main line status, and thus passing into the category which could be owned by a local authority.

Before actual electrification could begin, considerable work had to be undertaken. A flying junction was constructed just north of the station of Bourg-la-Reine, to avoid conflicting movements on the main line. All those platforms which had not yet been raised to full height (1.10m) were now so treated and on many stations canopies were extended to cover the full length of the platforms. All nine remaining level crossings were replaced by bridges and bridges or subways were constructed at all stations. An intermediate reversal point – which in the event was used for only a short time – was constructed at La Place and exchange facilities with the Métro were installed at Denfert-Rochereau.

A northbound train from Robinson is about to descend the flyunder built at Bourg-la-Reine for the electrification of the Sceaux line. *Brian Hardy*

The station of Arceuil-Cachan on line B is situated immediately south of the Acqueduc de la Vanne, which carries water from the River Loing to Paris. There has been an aqueduct on this site since Roman times, although the present structure dates from the mid-nineteenth century. A train of MI79 stock passes under the aqueduct and approaches the station, having just left the three-track section between there and La Place. Note the combined OPO mirror and monitor for the train operator and the digital clock – RER schedules are also calculated to a precision of five seconds, rather than half minutes. The station has scarcely been altered since built by the PO company and has now been repainted in the original colour scheme. *Brian Hardy*

In 1931 the interchange between the Sceaux line and the Petite Ceinture, formerly known as Sceaux-Ceinture, received a new station building and was renamed Cité Universitaire. As in other buildings on the RER, its features are emphasised by skilful use of modern lighting (November 1996). *Brian Patton*

Three new stations were constructed, at Bagneux, Parc de Sceaux and Fontaine-Michelon, while that at Sceaux-Ceinture had already, in 1930, been replaced by a new structure and renamed Cité Universitaire. A new station was constructed at the terminus of Massy-Palaiseau. At various stations, sidings were put in to act as refuges for the freight trains which would still run at off-peak times. A new depot and workshops complex was built at Montrouge, while a smaller depot at Massy housed a few trains and the electric locomotives which would work the freight traffic. All these works were executed in the years 1934–37, while ordinary traffic still operated. The smooth transition to electric operation was due in no small measure to Marc Langevin, who had overall responsibility for the conversion.

Massy-Palaiseau is a terminus for intermediate workings on line B. The train in the foreground has just reversed in the sidings beyond the station and a through service is seen on the right. On the far right is a train stabled in the sidings adjacent to Massy-Palaiseau depot. In the background is the former signal cabin, now closed, all signalling operations being controlled from the PCC at Denfert Rochereau. *Brian Hardy*

One of the Sceaux line electric locomotives, still in old livery, at the now-closed Montrouge depot on 26 November 1982. *Brian Hardy*

The line was electrified at 1500V dc, with overhead current collection. Unfortunately the CMP insisted on the use of certain standards of the Métro and as traffic developed, the distribution equipment was not always equal to its task. It was modified in the 1950s, after interruptions to service had reached unacceptable levels. The Z class rolling stock is fully described elsewhere.

The first electric trains ran, to steam train times, on 16 November 1937, between Luxembourg and Robinson. Service to Massy followed one week later, cross-platform interchange being provided to trains to and from Limours. Full service to the new timetable began on 18 January 1938, on which date the CMP assumed full control of its section. However, in 1936, the council of Seine-et-Oise had been authorised to borrow funds to allow electrification onwards to Saint-Rémy-lès-Chevreuse and public service on this section began, under SNCF auspices, on 3 December 1938, a diesel railcar connexion being offered to Limours. This latter section was closed to passengers on 15 May 1939. From 1 January of that year, the line was once again worked as a whole, regardless of ownership of the separate sections.

Despite some troubles in January 1938, when snow found its way into the motors of the new trains, the electrification scheme was a great success and passenger numbers almost immediately doubled and went on increasing to 18 million in 1939. The war of course brought record traffic and also, in June 1944, a few bombardments, in which the station of Massy-Verrières and two coaches were destroyed, as was the stock of spare rails. However, as staff who were members of the Resistance had hidden away a horde of 550 rails in a cranny at the city end of Port-Royal station, relaying was not a problem.

Passenger numbers soon began climbing again and when the line was incorporated into the RER in 1977, the annual total number was over 50 million. On 1 August 1964 the outer section was transferred to what was now RATP control. The main outward sign of this was the installation of automatic barriers at the level crossings which still existed on this stretch of line and the provision of footbridges or subways at stations. MS61 stock began to run on the line on 29 June 1967. Freight trains remained at the level of three per day until 1972, but thereafter there was a gradual reduction and these workings ceased in 1977.

When the line was electrified, a new and very individual signalling system was installed, to cope with passenger trains with high acceleration and also freight trains with rather different characteristics. Home signals were protected by two distant signals and all signals were repeated in the guard's cabin, backed by audible warning. The first distant signal showed three yellow lights when at danger, the second two and the home signal showed one or two red lights when at danger. The system worked well in practice and allowed a headway of 2.5 minutes between trains.

In 1969, when it was realised that the expense of two new north–south lines could not be contemplated, it was decided to utilise the Sceaux line as the basis of a new link and to extend it to Châtelet. Work began with the temporary closure of Luxembourg on 30 June 1974 and trial running over the new section, without passengers, began on 14 November 1977. With the opening for passenger service on 9 December of that year, the Sceaux line finally lost its separate identity and became line B of the RER.

THE NORTHERN SECTION

The original Gare du Nord was opened on 20 June 1846 by the Chemin de Fer du Nord, but the growth of traffic soon outstripped its facilities and the first of many rebuildings had to be undertaken in the 1860s. The present terminal building was opened in 1865 and its monumental façade has not since then been altered, although the interior has seen many changes and extensions, notably in 1875, 1889, the 1970s and at the present time. It was designed by Jakob Ignaz Hittorff, the preferred architect of Napoléon III, with the very active co-operation of the City of Paris. Suburban services developed considerably after 1918, although the Nord company tended to favour long-distance commuters rather than those from inner suburbs. Electrification was considered in the 1930s but not pursued, possibly because the Nord, with its steam tank engines of class 141TC and push-pull working, had brought steam operation to a level of excellence not known elsewhere. However, in conjunction with main line electrification, steam services out of Gare du Nord were converted to electric working, at 25kV ac, between 1958 and 1970. Further growth in traffic followed and in 1972 it was decided to build a new underground terminus for the lines to Mitry and Roissy; these works also allowed the construction of a new surface terminus for the other lines.

Class 141TC50, one of the powerful ex-Nord 2–8–2 tank locomotives, takes a refreshment break at Paris Nord in April 1968. These locomotives were designed by Marc de Caso and built between 1932 and 1935. The Cossard valve gear can be clearly seen. *Brian Patton*

In the original style of suburban livery, a four-car 88xx emu on line C arrives at Ermont Eaubonne in March 1994. Ermont Eaubonne is shared with SNCF services to and from Gare de Nord. *Brian Hardy*

The first line to operate out of Gare du Nord was that to Creil via Ermont, opened on 20 June 1846. On 3 June 1860, mainly as a result of inter-company rivalry, a new line was opened from a junction at La Plaine to Sevran and this was later extended to Soissons. Intended to give a direct route to Rheims, the line also developed a good deal of suburban traffic and its tracks were quadrupled as far as Aulnay-sous-Bois in 1913, when a flying junction with the main line was also opened. The line crossed the Grande Ceinture at Le Bourget, where extensive marshalling yards were constructed. In 1963 the quadruple tracks were extended to Villeparisis, with a third reversible track onwards to Mitry-Claye. The line was then resignalled and electrified. On 30 May 1976 a branch line, 13km in length, was opened from Aulnay to the airport of Roissy – Charles de Gaulle. Due to uncertainty about the location of future terminals, this station was located at some distance from the only operational terminal, access to which was by bus and, due to this inconvenience, the new branch did not attract as much airport traffic as had been expected.

LINE C

The history of the lines which were eventually united to form line C of the RER is extremely complicated, since these were built by three separate main line companies and they also include sections of both the Petite and Grande Ceintures.

THE WESTERN NETWORK

Contrary to the general philosophy of railway building in France, it was thought that Versailles was of such importance that it should be served by two railway lines and on 10 September 1840 the second line to the town was opened from a station at the Barrière du Maine, the predecessor of Montparnasse. It terminated at Versailles Rive-Gauche (RG). On 12 July 1849 this was linked at Viroflay (RG) to a newly opened line to Chartres and the west of France, with a station at Versailles Chantiers (CH). From 29 January 1852 both lines were worked as the Chemin de Fer de l'Ouest, a company formed with much British capital. This state of affairs was unacceptable to many French interests and in 1855, after prolonged negotiations, the Ouest was, as detailed above, amalgamated with various other companies, including the Saint-Germain company, to form the Chemins de Fer du Nord-Ouest, this being very soon shortened to 'Ouest', as stated above. Also in 1855 a double junction was constructed at Viroflay, which allowed trains form Saint-Lazare to work to any station in Versailles. In 1864 a branch to Dreux was opened, leaving the main line at Saint-Cyr. The company was constantly in financial difficulties and as a result tended to spend as little as possible on its infrastructure. The station at Versailles (CH) soon became a bottleneck, especially after the opening of the Grande Ceinture to Achères in 1882 and Juvisy in 1883. Suburban traffic began to develop from the 1880s, helped by the extension of weekly tickets to passengers in third class in 1884. This traffic had to be worked among main line trains to termini in Paris which had little spare capacity. Despite the then recent rebuilding of the station, the approach to Saint-Lazare remained a bottleneck and there were only two tracks from Montparnasse to Viroflay. The Ouest therefore decided in 1897 to construct an entirely new line, for both long-distance and suburban traffic, using an entry to Paris which was already under its control.

In the nineteenth century, Paris was noted for its international exhibitions, the first of which was held in 1855. That had been served only by horse buses and one tram line, but it was decided that the second, planned for 1867, should have access from the main line railways. To provide this, a short link of 3km was built from the Petite Ceinture at Point du Jour along the left bank of the Seine to Champ-de-Mars and was used by almost 1.5 million visitors to the exhibition. It was dismantled afterwards but a similar line was built from Grenelle to Champ-de-Mars to serve the 1878 exhibition and this remained in situ after that had closed. Both these lines had been worked by the Ouest, but access to them could be gained only over the tracks of the Ceinture and for the exhibition planned for 1889, the Ouest determined to use only its own metals. Using powers it had held since 1875, it extended the earlier line outwards to Issy-Plaine and Puteaux, over what is now tram line T2. This extension opened on 1 May 1889, with a service from Saint-Lazare to Champ-de-Mars.

The powers mentioned above also included an extension inwards towards the Pont de l'Alma, but because of its financial situation, the Ouest had shown no inclination to use these. However, as yet another exhibition was planned for 1900, the City of Paris prodded the company into an arrangement which was mutually beneficial. The City would make a free grant of the land necessary to extend the line inwards to a terminus, of appropriate architectural merit, on the Esplanade des Invalides. In return the railway company contributed 750,000 francs – half the total cost – towards the building of the Pont Alexandre III and undertook to replace the level crossings along the existing line by overbridges.

A declaration of public utility was obtained in 1893 and work then pressed ahead rapidly. However, to implement the plan mentioned above, a further declaration was obtained in 1897 for an extension outwards to Viroflay from Issy-Plaine. Another link also sanctioned at the same time was for a line over the Seine between Champ-de-Mars and Courcelles-Ceinture (raccordement de Boulainvilliers). The new network was to be completed by a line between Epone and Plaisir-Grignon, to allow trains from Brittany to gain access to the line to Invalides.

The pretty little station building at Javel was designed by Litsch and was originally erected at Champ-de-Mars to handle traffic to the 1889 exhibition. It has now been restored to its former elegance, as seen in March 1997. *Brian Patton*

A view on line C just south of Champ-de-Mars in June 1980, when class Z5300 units held undisputed sway. The original route that became the VMI line can be seen to the left and right of the track. *Brian Patton*

There were few problems with the extension from Champ-de-Mars to Invalides, most of which was in cutting and was in fact roofed over for the duration of the exhibition. The terminal building, designed by the architect Justin Litsch, was greatly admired and was considered to resemble an eighteenth-century orangerie. It contained at ground level only waiting rooms, some offices and the left luggage facilities, everything else being at a lower level. There were in all seven platforms and twelve lines. The Boulainvilliers link was also fairly easy to build, despite the built-up nature of the area traversed. But it was quite another matter with the line to Viroflay. This included a tunnel of 3.5km length immediately south of Meudon and construction of this was greatly delayed by a collapse of the workings.

A view looking south at Meudon – Val-Fleury in March 1997, with a class Z5300 set entering from the tunnel which caused so much trouble to the builders of the line. *Brian Patton*

Although there are modern station signs in plenty, the original and very handsome tiled name has been retained. *Brian Patton*

Because of the length and gradient of this tunnel (8mm/m), it had been decided to work the new line by electric traction, with 550V DC and third rail current collection. This was authorised on 8 September 1898 but by the beginning of 1900 it was clear that the rolling stock which had been ordered would not be ready for the opening of service in April of that year. Nor was the power station ready. The Ouest's engineers then set to work and within the time available produced a certain number – the exact figure has not survived – of what were described as 'trains automoteurs legers' (light railcar trains) of four coaches each, the two outer coaches being motored. The coaches were evidently of open saloon configuration, some accommodating 80 and some 90 passengers. The motors were 'found within the industry'. A temporary power station was constructed at Champ-de-Mars.

With all these problems, there must have been some nail-biting among senior management as the date for the opening of the new line and the exhibition approached. The lines and terminus were handed over with only four days to spare and there was no official opening ceremony. Some journalists were allowed to accompany the inspection train of 10 April 1900 and they were enthusiastic about the new trains, though enthusiasm was tempered by concern over a short-circuit, which caused a small fire with unpleasant fumes in the tunnel. One, prophetically, wrote that it would have been much worse in a crowded train. The disabled train was rescued by a steam locomotive.

The line from Courcelles to Champ-de-Mars was duly opened for service on 12 April but because of the fire mentioned above, the extension to Invalides was not opened until 15 April. Despite much publicity, the shuttle service of the 'automoteurs' from Champ-de-Mars to Invalides was virtually ignored by visitors to the exhibition, and at the annual general meeting of March 1901 the directors expressed themselves distinctly peeved about this – clearly they thought that the heroic last-minute efforts had not been appreciated. Perhaps the visitors had been too impressed by the intensive steam service, worked by 0–6–0 tanks over lines with manual signalling, to notice the little electric trains.

Electric service was opened to Meudon on 1 July 1901 and extended to Viroflay (RG) on 31 May 1902. The installations at Champ-de-Mars became in part a goods depot and in part a workshop for the electric trains. For once the Ouest had forgotten its usual parsimony and the extension illustrated all that was best in contemporary railway practice. The stations were well equipped, with handsome buildings lit by electricity. Current was supplied by a power station at Moulineaux and distributed by three substations. To avoid conflicting movements with the junction of the line to Montparnasse, a system of flying junctions was constructed at Porchefontaine.

Service was originally provided by one Thomson-Houston multiple unit train of eight coaches, two of which were motored, and one Sprague unit of nine coaches, of which three were motored. The motor coaches were carried on bogies, while the trailers were two-axle vehicles. The Thomson train had handsome clerestory coaches of very North American appearance, but it seems to have been unsuccessful in service, since it was de-motored in 1915. It could operate only as a complete unit. The Sprague train had an intermediate double-ended motor coach, allowing the operation of a five-coach train. It was of less attractive appearance but much more successful in service, since it was transferred in 1915 to the shuttle between Saint-Germain and Saint-Germain GC and lasted there until 1937. One of the motor coaches is now preserved in the Mulhouse museum. Both trains could achieve 60km/hr.

There were also ten 'fourgons moteurs' – in fact Bo-Bo electric locomotives with luggage space – of class 5000, which hauled ordinary stock of both compartment and saloon layout, and from 1924 main line trains.

These slightly exceeded their specifications, being able to haul 142 tonnes at 45km/hr on a gradient of 10mm/m. For pioneers they had a long life, eight lasting in traffic until 1951. For shunting within the confines of Invalides terminus, there were four bogie compressed air locomotives which proved to be unsuccessful and all had gone by 1910.

In May 1913, when a regular-interval service was introduced, most of the locomotive-hauled stock was replaced by 18 very luxurious and somewhat heavy all-metal multiple units, later known as the first series.

The preserved Sprague motor coach of 1901, beautifully restored to original condition, is a prized exhibit in the national railway museum in Mulhouse. *Brian Patton*

For the time, these were of advanced design, having four double sliding doors per side. These were joined in 1921 by 26 similar motor coaches, mounted on six-wheel bogies and weighing in at no less than 73 tonnes! These were known as the second series and were intended to be the first of 100 trains for the Saint-Lazare electrification but war had interrupted deliveries and the electrical equipment for the remaining 74 was ultimately used in the first batch of Standard stock. In service, both batches proved to be sluggish and were largely replaced by Standard stock between 1926 and 1928, when automatic signalling was introduced to the line and voltage was increased to 650V. However, they were not scrapped and in 1937 the First Series was converted to overhead working at 1500V dc and used on main line stopping services in motor-trailer formation. They did not finally disappear until 1973. The second series survived intact until 1948, when some were cut down to wagons and the remainder were put to work on the Issy-Puteaux shuttle until 1966. One of this series, TE1080, later Z23040, had been beautifully restored and is on display in the Mulhouse museum.

Despite its pioneering efforts, the Ouest/Etat still suffered from the constraint of double track between Clamart and Porchefontaine and by operating a mix of steam and electric trains. In 1928, under the presidency of Raoul Dautry, it was decided to modernise and rationalise the Left Bank lines. A new and much larger station at Versailles Chantiers was opened in 1932. All mainline trains were routed into Montparnasse in 1935 and in 1937 the line between that terminus and Le Mans was electrified at 1500V dc, with overhead current collection. To work semi-fast and outer suburban services, Budd stainless steel multiple units of a very advanced design (class Z23700) were introduced, these being the first application of this design in France. The Invalides line then settled down to a further 42 years of tranquil suburban existence.

A view, taken in March 1997, from platform level at Versailles Chantiers, showing the unusual signal cabin and the footbridge dating from the rebuilding of the station in 1932. *Brian Patton*

The reconstruction of the line out of Montparnasse in the 1930s saw the use of modern materials and some good instances of Art Deco design. This is the exterior of Versailles Chantiers in March 1997. *Brian Patton*

Unit Z23712, one of the articulated units ordered by the Etat for outer suburban service from Montparnasse stands at the latter station in June 1980. These units were very fast, one having attained 180km/hr on trial, although in service they were limited to 130km/hr. *Brian Patton*

THE VERSAILLES (CH) – MASSY LINE

This part of the Grande Ceinture was opened on 1 May 1883 and electrified in 1950. It is worked as part of line C, trains running from Versailles (CH) via Massy, Juvisy, Austerlitz and Issy to Versailles (RG), but it is not shown as part of the RER on line diagrams. In many places it still conveys the atmosphere of a rural branch line, with small stations and level crossings, but much housing development is taking place in the communities it serves and it is likely that it will become more of an urban line in the near future.

On the rural RER, a class Z5300 set approaches Vauboyen in March 1997, working from Versailles CH to Versailles RG, while a pedestrian happily takes a short cut beside the track! *Brian Patton*

THE SOUTH WESTERN LINES

The Chemin de Fer de Paris à Orléans, generally referred to as the PO, opened its first line from Paris to Corbeil on 20 September 1840. On 4 May 1843 this line was extended from a junction at Juvisy to Orléans and in 1865 a further main line was opened to Tours, leaving the original line at Brétigny. Local trains operated a sparse service to Étampes on the former and Dourdan on the latter. When weekly tickets were introduced, suburban traffic began to grow and to avoid saturation, the PO decided to quadruple the tracks as far as Brétigny, the outer tracks being given over entirely to suburban trains. A system of flying junctions kept the two streams of traffic clear of each other. The results, in terms of passenger numbers, were gratifying, as traffic increased by 20% between 1903 and 1905. The quadruple tracks were extended to Étampes in 1910 and a section of the Grande Ceinture between Choisy-le-Roi and Massy-Palaiseau was taken over by the PO on 27 August 1906.

However, improvements in the suburbs were not the only development planned by this company at the turn of the century. Its Paris terminus, Gare d'Austerlitz, is even today somewhat inconveniently located for the city centre and at that time also suffered from a restricted layout. Noting the recent agreement between the civic authorities and the Ouest (*q.v.*), the PO began to cast envious eyes on a site at Quai d'Orsay, occupied by the eyesore of buildings burned in the troubles of the Commune in 1871 but still not removed. This site was also restricted and access from Austerlitz could only be by a tunnel along the bank of the Seine, but it was a wonderfully central location. In 1897 agreement was reached on the purchase of the derelict buildings at a price of 11.5 million francs and on 29 November of the same year the PO obtained a declaration of public utility for an extension from Austerlitz to Quai d'Orsay. It then proceeded to construct an underground terminus of 16 tracks and eleven platform faces and, at surface level, a hotel of unparalleled splendour. The architect was Victor Laloux and, as befitted a building which faced the Louvre, this was of considerable distinction. It was also so constructed that light could penetrate to platform level.

As operation of this line by steam traction would have been difficult, some PO engineers were dispatched to the USA to study current practice in electric traction. Based particularly on the experience of the Baltimore and Ohio RR, they reported that it would be practicable to work not only suburban but also main line trains in this way and it was decided to use electric traction at 600V dc, with third rail collection in the tunnel and overhead in the station area, where the density of pointwork would have caused too much gapping with a third rail. Eight centre cab locomotives, known as 'boîtes à sel' (salt cellers) were bought from Blanc Misseron, with GEC electrical equipment, to work the extension, which in the event used a voltage of 550. These were numbered E1–E8 and most had a long life. E1, not withdrawn until 1966, is preserved in the Mulhouse museum. A limited service began on 28 May 1900 and full service for all trains was instituted at the end of July. For suburban trains, there was an intermediate station at Saint-Michel. The new line and stations were very well received and at its annual general meeting on 29 March 1901 the directors allowed themselves to boast that electric traction had functioned with regularity from the first day, without any trouble. Given that this was the first use of such traction with main line trains on this side of the Atlantic, their pride in the achievement is understandable and allowable!

On 1 July 1904 electric working of trains terminating at Juvisy was introduced, the outer two tracks being electrified. To work the suburban trains, three 'fourgons moteurs' were obtained, basically similar to the first batch but having end cabs. With two delivered at a later date, these were numbered E9–E13. There were also five double-ended motor coaches with seats for 32 passengers in third class, numbered AE1–AE5, with Thomson-Houston multiple unit equipment. Two more were obtained by 1913. Normally these worked in trains with seven two-axle coaches. To decrease dwell time at stations, the doors of the existing carriages were fitted with new locks, allowing them to be opened from inside and to engage automatically when closed.

This first electrification of an existing main line in France was brilliantly successful and traffic soared by 61% between 1903 and 1907. The branch from Choisy to Massy was electrified as far as Orly in 1921. This success encouraged the company to consider electrification of its main line. Progress was held up by the war, but in 1925 and 1926, the mainline and the Orly branch were converted to electric operation on the newly standardised system of 1500V dc with overhead current collection. In 1927 the line between Austerlitz and Quai d'Orsay was also converted to this system, the locomotives being altered accordingly. Eighty three-coach multiple unit trains replaced the compartment stock, but the earlier motor coaches were converted to the new system. Unfortunately the new trains were 'handed' and some of the trailers lacked driving cabs, so that electric working on the PO suburban services was not as flexible as it could have been. Nonetheless, the scheme was successful and additional stock had to be obtained in 1937. When these trains were replaced by modern stock in 1973, they migrated to the provinces for a further ten years service. Motor coach 23156 has been restored for preservation by Vitry workshop staff.

Unfortunately the growth of traffic also showed up the limitations of Quai d'Orsay and in the 1930s the number of main line trains using it was reduced. All such services ceased in 1939 and were not resumed after the war. Bereft of its main line traffic, the terminus gradually became rather run-down, but suburban traffic continued to grow and the introduction of class Z5300 stock from 1973 greatly simplified operation.

Traffic on the Massy branch beyond Orly was sparse and it was closed to passengers on 15 May 1939. Freight remained important, however, and this section was electrified on 6 February 1947. The creation of the airport of Paris Orly led to a reintroduction of passenger service as far as Pont de Rungis on 3 March 1969 and through to Massy on 25 September 1977.

Massy-Palaiseau is a large station complex and line C trains terminate a considerable distance from those of line B. In the line C bay platform a train has arrived from Montigny-Beauchamp. *Brian Hardy*

THE NORTH WESTERN LINES

In 1857 the Ouest and Nord companies signed an agreement to construct and work a joint line between Argenteuil on the former and Ermont on the latter. The reasons for this lie more with main line politics than suburban operation, but when the line was finally opened in 1863, a joint service, with double-deck stock of Ouest design, was instituted from Nord to Saint-Lazare via Ermont and Argenteuil. The service was reduced to a shuttle on the outbreak of war in 1914 and was then worked by rail motors of a curious design; the locomotive was placed between two carriages and to allow maximum visibility for the driver, the coach bodies were inset above the waistline in the direction of travel, the wider space below being used for luggage. These sets were nicknamed 'cages aux poules' (henhouses) and the service soon became known as 'la poule' (the hen). By the 1930s, the service had become the sole responsibility of the Nord, which used 141TC tank locomotives and standard push-pull stock. Diesel locomotives took over from 1969. In 1983 catenary was erected and electric service, still as a shuttle, began with the summer timetable of that year. At Ermont this line connected with the main line to Lille, opened on 20 June 1846. A more direct line was opened from Saint-Denis to Creil on 1 August 1863 and the old line thereafter saw only local traffic. On 21 May 1969 this line was electrified as far as Montigny-Beauchamp.

At Saint-Ouen – Garibaldi in August 1985 SNCF diesel BB66419 waits to propel a train of RIB stock to Ermont-Eaubonne. *Brian Patton*

Two years earlier the train is made up of rather work-weary ex-Etat Talbot stock of the early 1930s.
Brian Hardy

The Nord also incorporated in its suburban network another piece of industrial history. A small dock was established on the Seine at Saint-Ouen in 1830 and this was later linked to the Petite Ceinture at Epinettes by a short line opened in 1862. A passenger service was begun in 1868 and in 1889 the line was extended to Pont de Saint-Ouen. In 1908 this line was further extended to meet the Grande Ceinture at Ermont-Eaubonne, with a double junction at the latter point. While this link was intended mainly for freight, the stations were quite elaborate and passenger numbers gradually increased. The section to Pont de Saint-Ouen was closed in 1935. In 1969 diesel locomotives replaced the steam trains and in 1972 a new station at Saint-Ouen-Garibaldi gave a somewhat tortuous connexion to line 13 of the Métro. In 1977 service was cut back to terminate at this station, to allow work to proceed on alterations at Gare du Nord; at the same time the frequency was improved to a basic half-hourly service throughout the day. Traffic increased and the line's future was now assured. In 1981 a declaration of public utility incorporated it into the planning for the extension of line C.

THE PETITE CEINTURE

As the main line railways developed in the 1840s, they established in Paris not only passenger termini but also goods depots, these generally being located outside the then city boundary (roughly the course of lines 2 and 6 of the Métro). This was done to avoid paying the 'octroi', a tax levied on goods entering the city. As there were no rail links between those depots, they brought a considerable amount of heavy traffic on to the streets of what was still, in its layout, essentially a mediaeval city. Discussions were held about the possibility of providing rail links, but as the private companies were suspicious of one another, nothing was done, despite complaints from the business community.

All this changed abruptly in December 1851 when Louis Napoléon Bonaparte became President for life, becoming Emperor as Napoléon III just one year later. Only eight days after his coup d'état, a decree announced the construction of a circular line linking all main lines. This line was to run just inside the fortifications of the city, where it could also be of strategic value in the event of a siege. Each company was to contribute one million francs towards the cost of construction, which would be underwritten by the government. The line was to be worked by a syndicate of all main line companies serving the capital.

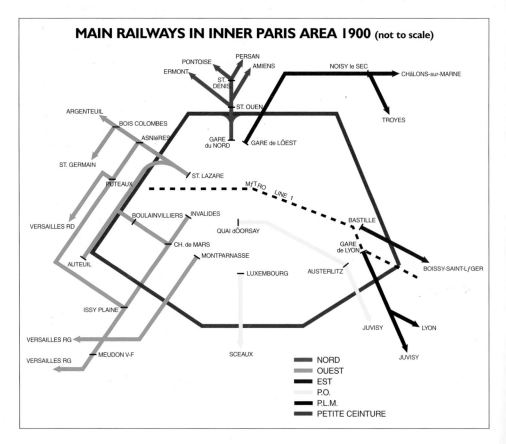

40

Construction went ahead quickly and the first section, from Batignolles to Pont du Nord was opened for traffic on 15 November 1852. The next section included some extensive tunneling at Charonne and Belleville and was opened to Bercy and across the Seine to a junction with the PO line at Ivry on 25 March 1854. At this time, only goods trains were operated, apart from troop specials and emigrant trains. The line prospered and by 1860 was carrying a million tonnes of goods traffic per year. There was also much industrial development along its length and the syndicate opened some goods depots on its own account.

The Ceinture Rive-Gauche was authorised by a declaration of public utility on 14 June 1861 and opened on 25 February 1867. It ran from Auteuil to Ivry and at the former connected with the Auteuil line of the Ouest. The circle was completed on 25 March 1869 when a link was opened between Courcelles on the Auteuil line and Clichy.

The original decree had envisaged the provision of a passenger service but the operating companies showed little enthusiasm for this and it was only by ministerial decree of 14 August 1861 that preparations for a passenger service were actually begun. The lack of enthusiasm was reflected in the spartan nature of the stations. Service began on 14 July 1862 and at first passenger numbers were low, to the point where some trains operated as mixed trains. But by 1878 the Ceinture was carrying five million passengers per year. Double-deck coaches of Ouest design were used. Freight traffic became less important after the opening of the Grande Ceinture, completed in 1886. In 1892 and 1893 connecting lines were opened to Gare du Nord and a service was instituted from that station.

The year 1900 probably marked the apogee of the Ceinture as a passenger line. To the basic service of four trains per hour (six on Sundays and holidays), were added the services to Gare du Nord, from Saint-Lazare to Auteuil and to Champ-de-Mars and from the latter to Courcelles via Vincennes. In that year, 339 million passengers were carried. The double-deck stock had been replaced by more modern compartment coaches and to work these trains, the syndicate used a series of handsome compound 4–6–0 tank locomotives, with their cylinders placed, unusually, in tandem.

But the opening of the first line of the Métro had already doomed the Ceinture's passenger traffic, which fell alarmingly to 14 million passengers in 1913 and seven million in 1927. The circular service was cut during the war and not reinstated afterwards, trains operating from Courcelles to Auteuil via Ivry. No attempt was made to counter the decline, other than by reducing frequencies, and all stations were still fully manned. The syndicate considered offering the line to the CMP but the latter showed no interest and replied that it would consider taking it over only after electrification and construction of links with the Métro. This was not likely to be sanctioned by the main line companies and the only alternative was closure. After some legal wrangling, the last train ran on 23 July 1934, the service being replaced by the PC bus service. It was a great pity that Paris should have lost this link, just at a time when the electric service on the Ring in Berlin had shown how modern traction and operating methods could revitalise a comparable line.

The northern part of the Ceinture continued to be used for inter-station movements and stock transfers until recent years, although these have now almost ceased. The southern portion has been abandoned but part will be reactivated in future as a tram line. A short portion of its trackbed was used as a test track for recent deliveries of stock to the Métro.

THE AUTEUIL LINE

This part of line C has been mentioned several times in passing but it is of such historical importance that it deserves a section to itself.

In 1852 the Saint-Germain company decided to build a line from Batignolles to Auteuil, mainly with a view to spreading its fixed costs over a wider base. This line was probably the first in the world to be built through a district which was already almost completely developed, to serve the internal traffic flows of a city, rather than connecting separate towns. It was intended to provide a frequent service, probably with a view to capturing some of the omnibus traffic in the area, and at week-ends it was expected that there would be substantial pleasure traffic to the newly opened Bois de Boulogne. In short this line was the world's first urban métro, though the term was not used at the time. The line opened for traffic on 2 May 1854, just before the Saint-Germain company was absorbed, on favourable terms, by the Chemins de Fer de l'Ouest.

The line was at first operated on a half-hourly headway, increased on Sundays and holidays to one of twenty minutes. Fares were low and season tickets were available from the beginning. The public responded eagerly to the new service, which was soon one of the most profitable parts of the system.

In 1867 trains of the Petite Ceinture began to use the line, which then saw a train every ten minutes in each direction. Unfortunately, as part of this operation, the original high platforms were reduced in height. The line suffered considerable damage in the troubles of the Commune in 1871, but once matters returned to normal, it prospered again. With the addition of trains to and from Gare du Nord, the line was by 1894 working very near the limits of its capacity and in that year was used by over 22 million passengers.

As part of the preparations for the exhibition of 1900, it was decided to quadruple the tracks between Courcelles and Passy. Work began in 1897 and, without any interruption to the service, was completed in April 1900. That year marked the high point of the line's history, with special trains for distinguished visitors in addition to the passenger service from Saint-Lazare to Champ-de-Mars. The special trains used the station then known as Avenue du Bois de Boulogne, formerly Avenue de l'Impératrice and since 1929 Avenue Foch. The use of this station for such purposes continued for many years afterwards, the last occasion being that of the visit to Paris by George VI and the present Queen Mother in 1938, when a streamlined pacific of the Nord, painted blue and adorned with the Union Jack brought the royal couple to Paris.

At one time, the Ouest provided buffet cars on some of its suburban services and between 1899 and 1902 this facility was extended to the Auteuil line. The cars were operated by the Compagnie Francaise des Wagons-Buffets. Apparently the hot chocolate was delicious, but the length of even the longest journey possible on the line could hardly have allowed time for it to cool before it was drunk! The 'Wagons Bars' which were used were two-axle teak bodied coaches, scaled down versions of main line dining carriages. In the event their use on the Auteuil line proved to be unprofitable and they were soon deployed elsewhere, much to the relief of the temperance lobby, which had actively campaigned against them. They were finally withdrawn in 1914.

After 1900, the line lost some passengers to the Métro and the electric trams, and the opening of line 9 of the former was fatal to the shuttle to Champ-de-Mars, which closed on 1 June 1924. But the frequent service and good access to Saint-Lazare meant that a reasonable level of traffic could be maintained and it was therefore included in the plans for electrification, which took place on 2 January 1925. However, the electric trains ran only a shuttle service from Pont Cardinet. Service settled down to a twenty minute headway at off-peak times, this being doubled in peak periods. By 1934 a ten minute headway was being run throughout the day until 20.30. The fare structure was aligned to that of the Métro, but without the benefit of through tickets.

The line survived the war more or less intact, though the link to the Ceinture Rive-Gauche was severed by a bomb in 1944 and not reinstated afterwards. These years also saw a most unusual set in service on the line – an articulated three-coach train running on pneumatic tyres. The body was of lightweight aluminium and weighed only 32 tonnes. Unfortunately it was badly damaged by fire on 11 August 1943 and was not rebuilt after the war. This set, ZBEyf 23271, was the predecessor of all rubber tyred trains on the Metro today.

For a time after the war, the Auteuil line had a rather run-down appearance, but in 1968 interchange at Pont Cardinet was improved to allow cross-platform interchange with trains from Saint-Lazare, while in 1971–72, a programme of renovation of stations in their original style was carried through. Thereafter, there was another period of calm until, to the regret of many regular passengers, the last train of Standard stock left Pont Cardinet on the snowy night of 6/7 January 1985 and the line closed for rebuilding, prior to incorporation into line C of the RER.

A two-car train of Standard stock awaits departure from Auteuil-Boulogne on 11 February 1982.
Brian Hardy

THE SOUTHERN SECTION

Very considerable difficulties surrounded the building of the terminal station for the Paris-Lyon main line and the company originally formed to operate it went bankrupt in 1848. It was therefore taken over by the government of the newly created Second Republic, which completed the works and opened the first section from Paris Gare de Lyon to Tonnerre on 12 August 1849. The line was handed back to private enterprise, in the form of the new Paris-Lyon-Mediterranée company (PLM) on 5 January 1852. This company very definitely saw itself as a long-distance railway and was often called 'La Ligne Impériale'. It had very little interest in suburban traffic and the first Gare de Lyon had no facilities for this. However, in 1878, two new platforms, located in the space between the arrival and departure platforms, were opened to cater for local services. Both suburban and long distance traffic continued to grow in a satisfactory manner and in 1891 the management of the PLM decided on a complete reconstruction of the station, with a new terminal building in keeping with the status of the line. Having briefly toyed with the idea of a two-level station, the PLM settled for one of 13 platforms on one level, designed by the architect Marius Toudoire, who had already designed St Jean station in Bordeaux. The works proved again to be difficult but were finally completed in 1901, when the present monumental complex was opened. The cost was 20 million francs, or about £2 million at contemporary rates of exchange.

Further expansion led to the construction of eight new platforms in 1927, to which main line departures were transferred, suburban traffic remaining in the former station. Electrification from 1951 onwards rendered even this arrangement inadequate and, with the construction of line A of the RER, the opportunity was taken to build a new underground station of four tracks, initially as a terminal, for suburban traffic. This station was opened on 28 September 1980.

When the underground station at Gare de Lyon opened in 1980, it was for some years a terminus, until new tunnels to Châtelet were completed and opened in 1995. The platforms are extremely long and can easily accommodate ten-car trains of double-deck 'Interconnexion' stock.
Brian Hardy

Unit Z5173 stands at Montparnasse in June 1980 after arrrival from Rambouillet. This unit belonged to the second batch of class, Z5100 delivered in 1957 for use on the lines of the western area. *Brian Patton*

The original line followed, for most of its length, the valley of the Seine as far as Montereau, the present-day terminus of suburban traffic. This section was actually opened in advance of the terminal station, on 3 January 1849 and from the start was double track throughout. Tracks as far as Villeneuve-Saint-Georges, which had in the meanwhile become a junction of some importance, were quadrupled between 1881 and 1884 and two further tracks were installed between 1901 and 1904. These were used in common by all trains and there were no dedicated suburban lines. The pleasant nature of the area led to the building of much middle class housing and to cope with increasing suburban traffic, quadruple tracks were extended to Brunoy in 1906 and to Combs-la-Veille-Quincy in 1913. Finally quadruple tracks reached Melun in 1921. This station is now the terminus of line D, as well as being a traffic centre of some importance in its own right, with a fair amount of commuter traffic from other towns in the area. The line was electrified, at 1500V dc, on 29 August 1950, when new stations were opened at Yerres and Le Mée; traffic grew considerably, despite the initial use of old rolling stock and elderly ex-PO locomotives. Other new stations at Grigny, Grand-Bourg and Essonnes-Robinson were opened soon afterwards and electric multiple units of class Z5100 arrived in 1954 to provide a more modern travelling environment.

A branch line was opened from Villeneuve-Saint-Georges to Juvisy on 18 May 1863. There it linked with a line to Corbeil, which had been opened by the PO company on 20 September 1840. This was now transferred to the PLM and a new station was opened at Corbeil. A link to Melun was opened for traffic on 1 June 1897, when a new spur from the latter to Montereau via Héricy was also commissioned. This line was also electrified on 29 August 1950 and again several new stations were built.

To serve the new town of Evry, a spur was built from this line between Grigny – Val-de-Seine and Corbeil. It was opened as far as Grigny-Centre on 15 February 1974 and extended to Corbeil on 6 December 1975. Gradients on this line are severe, but it is normally served only by multiple unit trains. With many tunnel sections and closely spaced stations, it has something of the character of a métro.

A branch line, originally single track, was opened from Corbeil to Malesherbes and on to Montargis on New Year's Day 1865. Track was later doubled, but was singled again beyond Malesherbes in 1955, when this section lost its passenger service. The line as far as La Ferté-Alais, which is situated on the boundary of Ile-de-France and is the terminus of the other branch of line D, was electrified at 1500V dc on 21 January 1984, when through trains to Paris were instituted. The outer section was similarly electrified on 27 September 1992.

Finally it should be mentioned that the PLM was linked to the Grande Ceinture at Villeneuve-Saint-Georges by a line from Noisy-le-Sec in 1877 and by a line towards Versailles in 1883.

THE NORTHERN SECTION

The direct line from Saint-Denis to Creil via Orry-la-Ville was opened by the Nord company on 1 June 1859. (Other sources give the date as 10 May.) It was double track throughout and was quadrupled to La-Chapelle-en-Serval in 1907, the new lines being intended for main line trains only. The line was linked to the Grande Ceinture in 1884 and in 1993 was also linked to the TGV Nord between Villiers-le-Bel and Goussainville. Electrification, at 25kV AC, took place on 9 December 1958, this being the first use of high voltage equipment in the area.

The station building of Villiers-le-Bel is typical of those built by the Nord company. On 18 February 1988 a train of line D, made up of units of class Z8800, is seen; these units have since been replaced on this line by class Z20500. *Brian Hardy*

46

THE NORTHERN SECTION

The terminus of the Strasbourg company, later the Chemins de Fer de l'Est, at Gare de l'Est, was opened on 5 July 1849, although not fully completed until three years later. The architect was Francois Duquesney, who believed firmly that the function of a station should be clearly indicated by its architecture. It says much for his concept that, alone among Paris termini, this station still preserves its original outline, despite much enlargement and rebuilding in the intervening years. The initial two platforms had increased to 16 by 1912, in which year the Est decided on a complete rebuilding. Due to the outbreak of war, the project was delayed, but was made more necessary by the increase in traffic which followed the recovery of Alsace and Lorraine by France in 1918. Finally in 1928 work began and was completed on 23 December 1931. There were now 30 platform faces, of which the twelve easternmost were reserved for suburban traffic. This continued to grow but electrification, at 25kV ac, inaugurated on 22 May 1962, enabled the station to keep pace with the demands placed on it until recent years.

The first line of the company was to Strasbourg. Originally double track throughout, successive enlargements were made over the years to 1916. Today there are six tracks as far as Noisy-le-Sec and four tracks onwards to Lagny, but there is an additional track between Noisy and Bondy. From Lagny to Meaux, terminus of the suburban service, there is double track. This section was opened for traffic on 5 July 1849. A branch from Esby to Crécy-la-Chapelle was brought into use on 11 July 1902. This section was electrified on 29 May 1980. It was originally planned that this line would be extended to Coulommiers, but Crécy has remained its terminus.

A class Z22500 unit, bearing the appropriate headcode HOLE, heads towards Paris through the complex of lines at Noisy-le-Sec in July 1999. *Brian Patton*

This illustration of cross-platform interchange at Bondy in July 1999 provides an interesting contrast between elderly RIB stock on the shuttle train to Aulnay-sous-Bois on the left and the new stock of line E on the right. *Brian Patton*

On 7 July 1856 a branch, the first part of the line to Mulhouse in Alsace, was opened from Noisy as far as Nogent-le-Perreux and this was extended in stages to Provins, reached on 11 December 1858. A branch from Gretz to Coulommiers was opened in stages between 1861 and 2 April 1863 and today suburban trains operate on this line as far as Tournan. This part of the line was electrified on 13 December 1973. Until recently there has been much interchange traffic with line A at Val-de-Fontenay. Due to the continuing growth of population, electrification was carried on to Coulommiers on 24 January 1992, with a good service of outer-suburban trains being provided in peak hours.

From Bondy, on the line to Meaux, a separate company opened what was essentially a steam tramway to Aulnay-sous-Bois on 8 September 1875. The line was not a financial success and was taken over by the state, to be assigned to the Est company in 1883. There was a link to the tracks of the Nord at Aulnay and until 1930 a circular service was operated from Gare de l'Est to Gare du Nord via this route. Over the years the line lost some, but by no means all of its tramway character and additional stations and halts were opened. Electrification reached Gargan on 22 May 1982 and Aulnay on 26 September 1977. With much roadside reservation and also some tramway-style central reservation, it still remains an interesting byway in the Ile-de-France network.

THE SOUTH WESTERN SECTION

It is intended that line E will ultimately incorporate the service at present operated from Saint-Lazare to Saint-Nom-la-Bretèche. This branch from Saint-Cloud was opened on 5 May 1884. The line was constructed by the state, though operated by the Ouest company, and the station buildings are very similar to those of stations on the Grande Ceinture, to which the line was linked at its terminus. Originally a circular service was operated from Saint-Lazare to Saint-Lazare via Saint-Nom and Versailles Chantiers, but this did not attract much traffic and from 1889 branch trains ran to Saint-Germain GC. However, the cash-strapped Ouest disliked paying tolls for the use of the Ceinture tracks and from 1894 most trains terminated at Saint-Nom, the link to Saint-Germain being finally severed in 1914.

Electrification reached Saint-Nom-la-Bretèche on 15 May 1931. This was converted to 25kV ac as far as Garches on 16 September 1977 and on to the terminus on 15 September 1978. Service is currently provided by single-deck units of class Z6400.

The other line which may be incorporated into line E is that to Versailles Rive-Droite (RD). This was built by an offshoot of the Saint-Germain company, from whose line it diverged at Asnières, and was opened on 4 August 1839. The line ran along one side of the royal (later imperial) park of Saint-Cloud and the company was obliged to erect a decorative screen along this stretch and also contribute to the civil list! Until 1870 there was also a private station at Saint-Cloud. The line was amalgamated with the first Cheimin de Fer de l'Ouest in 1851. Electrification reached Becon-les-Bruyères on 27 April 1924 and Versailles on 22 July 1928. Conversion to 25kV ac followed in the 1970s, reaching Saint-Cloud on 15 September 1976 and Versailles on 16 September 1977. Interchange with line A is provided at La Défense, where the original modest station has grown to one of six tracks, two of which are used by trams, with good links to roads and motorways.

Since entering service, SNCF units of class Z22500 have acquired a blue band below the windscreen with the Transilien logo. A unit of class Z22500 heads inbound to Haussmann at Les Bouillereaux Champigny in July 2000.
Brian Patton

THE DEVELOPMENT OF THE RER

The first tentative proposals for a regional métro were made in the 1920s, in response to the growth of the suburban area. The CMP (then operator of the urban system) was aware of the need to extend its services beyond the former gates of the city and the main line railways were now much more co-operative, having become somewhat disillusioned with suburban operation and its accompanying deficits. The way was therefore open for a co-ordinated approach. The first proposals were published in 1927 and involved the Sceaux and Vincennes lines; the former was to be extended inwards to Saint-Michel while the latter was to be linked to line 1 of the Métro. The Invalides–Versailles (RG) line was also to be linked to line 10. Fortunately these plans were not put into effect, but another plan of the same year, drawn up by E Jayot, proposed using both the Saint-Germain and Vincennes lines as the basis of an east–west link and the Sceaux line, extended to Le Bourget in the north, as a north–south axis. This would connect at Massy-Palaiseau with an extension of the planned line 14 of the Métro. The CMP was enthusiastic and it was from this plan that the electrification of the Sceaux line was developed. The CMP engineer in charge of that project was Marc Langevin and he became convinced of the importance of such links. In 1936 the CMP put forward another plan, drawn up by Langevin and H Ruhlmann, for a regional system of three lines, basically the present lines A, B and C but also including the line to Saint-Nom-la-Bretèche. Several study groups from the CMP had visited London and as a result all ideas of inter-working with the urban system had gone. The new lines were to be built to main line loading gauge and to allow an average speed of 50km/hr. A link from the Petite Ceinture would allow freight trains to run to Les Halles.

Langevin may be considered the father of the RER, just as Bienvenüe was the father of the urban Métro. A graduate of the École Polytechnique, he was recruited as an engineer by the CMP in 1928. After his work with the Sceaux line, he served in the army in 1939–40 and later, unusually for a manager of the CMP, joined the Resistance. In November 1944 he was made director of the traction section and very shortly afterwards became interim manager of the rail network, and general manager in 1953. He retired in 1960.

The outbreak of war put a stop to all plans for future expansion but the Vichy government, in the Law of 4 June 1941, created a unitary tariff for all transport in the Paris area, based on that already in operation on the Sceaux line. Post-war reconstruction had to take precedence over these plans but Langevin ensured that RATP did not forget the idea of a regional express system. The plans were discussed again in 1955 and 1959. On the latter occasion, the new government of de Gaulle took note, seeing in the proposals a way of serving the new business centre to be built at La Défense, and finally in 1961 agreed to set aside the sum of two million (new) francs to finance the construction of an underground line from there to Nation, with a link to the Saint-Germain line at Nanterre. In 1963 it was decided to transfer the Vincennes line to RATP and link it to the new line.

LINE A – SUCCESS AGAINST THE ODDS

A symbolic ground-breaking ceremony was held at Neuilly on 6 June 1961, but this did not immediately result in great progress. Perhaps because Langevin was no longer in charge, perhaps because the plans had been so long in the making, the final quick authorisation seems to have taken RATP by surprise. No detailed planning had been undertaken. Despite what was known about the subsoil of Paris, only two trial borings were made and the exact route of the tunnels through the central area was still not decided when work began in 1961. Tunnelling was started at both La Défense and Étoile. The shield developed by the firm of Campenon-Bernard proved to be unsuitable for use in such widely varying subsoil and even by 1964 only 500m of tunnel had been completed.

The slow progress, the escalation of costs far above the original estimates and a disparity between payments authorised and actual expenditure caused something of a crisis in the affairs of RATP. The government commission of audit had a good deal to say about the lack of proper budgeting and remarked that the initial studies had been insufficient. In December 1963 the Minister of Transport dismissed the Director-General of RATP, and in his place appointed Pierre Weil, External Relations Officer of SNCF. The reorganisation which Weil then implemented within RATP, and in particular the creation of a Department of New Works, made possible a much more energetic approach to the building of line A within a realistic time scale and ensured that RATP would henceforth recruit staff of the necessary calibre for such an operation. It was decided to complete first the re-electrification of the Saint-Germain line with its link to the new tunnel section, itself to be extended to Auber, and the electrification of the Vincennes line, before beginning work on the central area tunnel.

In 1964 the unsatisfactory shield was replaced by a 'Robinson' excavator, with which much better progress was made. To speed matters up, Weil also decided to take the line under the Seine by submerged caissons, rather than the tunnel originally planned. In 1965 the plans were assimilated into the overall plan of the Schéma Directeur. In the same year, excavations caused decompression which led to the collapse of part of the tunnel of line 1 of the Métro, on which service had to be suspended for four days. There was also a spectacular incident when a column of pyrite ignited spontaneously after being exposed to compressed air. Thereafter matters improved and the tunnel was completed by January 1968.

Meanwhile in the east, work was going ahead on the Vincennes line, which gave rather fewer problems than the western sector. Tunnelling began at Nation in September 1965 and the new line was opened for traffic by Pierre Weil on 12 December 1969. The section between Saint-Mandé and Bastille was abandoned and replaced by the tunnel link to Nation. The terminus at Bastille, after serving for a time as an exhibition centre, was demolished to make way for the new opera house. The closure of the inner stations led to a transfer of passengers to line 1 of the Métro.

Apart from the tunnelling, much work was undertaken to reconstruct stations on both lines, and interchange facilities with road transport received particular attention. Track and signalling had to be renewed or adapted for the higher speeds envisaged and the last two level crossings on the Vincennes line were replaced by bridges. RER tracks were completely separated from those still to be used by SNCF trains. A new depot was constructed at Boissy-Saint-Léger.

A class MS61 set in anti-graffiti livery is in the underground terminus of Saint-Germain-en-Laye.
Brian Hardy

In the west a shuttle service was inaugurated on 20 February 1970 between Étoile and La Défense, after some preliminary running during an exhibition in January. This was extended inward to Auber on 23 November 1971, the vast station at the latter point having been officially opened by President Pompidou three days earlier. This was the first occasion on which the head of state had actually opened an urban rail link, though President Doumergue had once visited the Métro workshops of line 9. Finally the line was completed through to Saint-Germain and service began on 1 October 1972. The reconstruction of this line had been rather more difficult than that of the Vincennes line, since with third rail electric trains still running during the process, very strict safety precautions had been necessary. The viaduct by which the second crossing of the Seine was made at Croissy had been completely rebuilt. There had been considerable delays (caused by government indecision over the siting of the museum of the twentieth century) in the building of the new station at Nanterre-Préfecture and in the reconstruction of Rueil workshops, which SNCF did not vacate until 1968. A new station, the fourth in the line's history, was built at Le Pecq. In view of all these problems, the opening ahead of schedule reflected great credit on all concerned.

When the original plans for a regional system had been drawn up by Langevin, it was envisaged that the east–west and north–south lines would intersect at Etienne Marcel. However, when the project was officially adopted in 1959, it was decided that the connexion should be made at Châtelet. As mentioned above, the building of the central link was postponed and it was not until October 1970 that the Cabinet decided that it should be completed. This decision did not in the event lead to any construction, since the future of this line had become entangled with much wider issues.

When construction was first proposed, it was suggested by the local authorities that it would be sensible to build an underground suburban station at Gare de Lyon along with that for the RER. This would relieve the main line station of some of its suburban traffic and allow more space for the facilities which would be necessary for the new TGV service. But from this stemmed the idea of inter-connecting these suburban services with the RER and running them through to Gare du Nord, using an enlarged interchange at Châtelet. Not surprisingly, this proposal caused a good deal of opposition. Environmentalists feared (correctly) that it would lead to a concentration of office development around the new station. The Finance Minister, Giscard d'Estaing, soon to be President, queried the escalation of costs from 1,050 million francs to 3,200 million, although it was pointed out that the fixed costs could be spread more widely under this scheme. Pierre Weil was totally against through running. Apart from the technical problem of different voltages, he correctly foresaw problems of overcrowding on the central portion of the lines concerned. But the idea had gained the approval of certain ministers, notably Jacques Chaban-Delmas, and when a study visit to Tokyo (where such through running is common practice) was arranged, Weil was excluded. Clearly his position had become untenable and he resigned in December 1971. It was a sadly premature end to the career of a man who had done so much for rail transport.

Weil's successor, Pierre Giraudet had been (like Bienvenüe) an engineer in the department of Roads and Bridges and immediately before coming to RATP, he had been Director-General of Le Bourget airport. He did not break altogether with the policies of his predecessor, but altered their direction and made the re-establishment of good relations with SNCF his priority. During 1972 a joint working party resolved the technical problems and finally in November 1972 the government gave its approval to the construction of the central portion of line A, with interconnexion with line B at Châtelet and the extension of the latter to Gare du Nord and beyond over the tracks of SNCF.

The task of building 5.5km of line in tunnel across the centre of Paris was clearly not going to be easy but the technical services of the authorities involved had already begun to make plans, in anticipation of authorisation being given and it was possible to start work almost at once. The most complex operations centred around the building of the stations of Châtelet – Les Halles and Gare de Lyon and for more than twenty months Parisians had to put up with living with one of the world's largest ever holes, as the site of the former station was excavated. The subsoil was anything but homogenous. Nevertheless work went ahead as planned and when the Robinson excavator broke through into the station site on 13 January 1975, it was found that the alignment of the tunnel to the station was out by exactly one centimetre! Operations at Gare de Lyon were equally complex and made more risky by the presence of the tower with the station clock, whose total weight was estimated at 6,000 tonnes. Again, however, work went ahead without any serious problems. In the layout of this station,

RER line A in the Marne Valley opened in three stages and all of it was new construction. A typical station of the late 1970s is Neuilly Plaisance, seen on 7 May 1994. *Brian Hardy*

not only were facilities provided to allow for future inter-running with SNCF, but provision was also made for a possible future diversion of Métro line 8 towards Bercy and a deviation of line 5; the works carried out for the former have in fact been used in the building of line 14. The excavation of the tunnel itself was relatively easy. Work was carried out from four shafts and the Robinson excavator progressed at an average rate of 28m per day. The through line was opened for public service on 9 December 1977, though the SNCF suburban station was not ready until 28 September 1980.

Much of the development of the RER in the suburbs is connected with the building of five new towns, first proposed in the Schéma Directeur of 1965. These were to be located at Marne-la-Vallée (east), Cergy-Pontoise (north west), Saint-Quentin-en Yvelines (west), Evry (south) and Melun-Senart (south east). These were to be linked to Paris and to each other by a modern railway system, which would also serve the city's two airports, and this seems to have been the first official use of the term Réseau Express Régional. Line A would serve the first two.

In the east, work was begun in 1971 on a branch of line A to serve Marne-la-Vallée, which was planned in such a way that three-quarters of the inhabitants would live no more than 800m from a station. The branch would leave the existing line just before Fontenay-sous-Bois and run mostly on the surface with a crossing of the Marne by viaduct. There was a good deal of local opposition to this surface course and many politicians urged that the line should be built entirely in tunnel. Alarmed, RATP undertook an extensive campaign of public relations, which greatly lessened the opposition, and also took especial care with the design of the stations. The branch was officially opened on 8 December 1977 when President Giscard d'Estaing – who seemed to have forgotten his earlier opposition to the RER – took the controls of a unit of MS61 stock and drove it through to the provisional terminus of Noisy-le-Grand. The train was followed by an SNCF autorail in case of incident, but fortunately the President showed himself to be a competent driver and it was not required. The inaugural train then returned to Châtelet, where he formally opened the station, mentioning that the government had contributed a total of 2.3 milliard francs to the building of the RER. Public service began on 10 December. The line was extended to its terminus at Torcy on 19 December 1980. On 31 March 1992 it was extended a further 11km to a terminus at Chessy, which was intended to serve the newly opened Eurodisney 'leisure park'. There is also interchange at this point with the tangential line of the TGV.

Unfortunately matters did not run so smoothly in the west. One of the new lines proposed was to run from Saint-Quentin-en-Yvelines to Cergy, passing through La Défense. The government, anxious to present a modern image of France to the rest of the world, decided to build the line from there to Cergy not as a conventional railway but as an Aérotrain. This was a form of high-speed monorail developed by the engineer Jean Bertin (who was also, none too successfully, involved with hovercraft), which had already attained a speed of 422km/hr on a test track. The system was to use linear-induction motors, which were then far from a commercial proposition, and the firm which was developing them had in 1974 to be rescued by Jeumont-Schneider, whose staff estimated that another three years' work would be necessary before even a prototype could be tested. The coaches would be 16m long and only 2m wide and be capable of a maximum speed of only 100km/hr. These would have run on a line built on T-shaped supports, which would have been visually very obtrusive, at a height of 5m above the ground. It was planned to run non-stop between Cergy and La Défense, totally ignoring intermediate traffic, and the capacity of the line would have been greatly inferior to a conventional one using MS61 stock. Finally in July 1974, when the estimated cost of the line had reached 600 million francs, as against 230 million for a conventional line, the government had the courage to admit its mistake and the concept was abandoned, thus sparing Parisians a good deal of inconvenience.

The end of line A is Marne-la-Vallée, reached in 1992, when the Eurodisney resort opened. This view of the island platform station looks towards the end of the line, where there are four sidings for stabling trains. On the right the TGV station can be seen under construction. *Brian Hardy*

Above A six-car train of MS61 stock in Ile-de-France livery arrives at Nanterre Université on a dismal summer's day in 1998. On the right out of the picture are the SNCF lines to and from Saint-Lazare, while the Cergy/Poissy branch of line A passes over on the viaduct. *Brian Hardy*

Opposite, top The first station beyond Nanterre Préfecture on the 1987–88 extension of line A on to SNCF metals is Houilles – Carrières-sur-Seine, still shared with SNCF suburban services. An eight coach train of class MI84 stock is seen after arrival. *Brian Hardy*

Opposite, bottom In contrast to earlier stations on line A, that at Cergy le Haut, opened in 1994, makes good use of natural light and the entrance is inviting. *Brian Hardy*

In its place, the government agreed to the construction of a new SNCF line, using a freight-only branch from Achères on the line to Poissy, with some new construction in Cergy itself. There would also be a new spur at Nanterre, to allow a connexion to be made with line A at Nanterre-Université. Rebuilding of the freight line went ahead rapidly, as did the new construction, and the line was opened for traffic on 29 March 1979, with a through service to Saint-Lazare. It was extended over new tracks to Cergy-Saint-Christophe on 26 September 1985. It had always been the intention that this line, as well as that to Poissy, should be taken over by line A, but the difficulties experienced on the latter in the 1980s (*q.v.*) meant that this had to be postponed until 29 May 1988 for the Cergy line and 20 May 1989 for that to Poissy. These lines were electrified at 25kV ac and trains change voltage immediately after leaving Nanterre-Préfecture, where RATP drivers hand over to those of SNCF. Work was begun in 1990 on a further 2km extension to Cergy le Haut and this was opened on 29 August 1994 with a new intermediate station at Nouvelle Université. A peak hour only service to Saint-Lazare is still maintained.

THE PROBLEM OF SUCCESS

The construction of line A was a magnificent technical achievement which gave Paris a cross-city link which other less fortunate capitals can only envy. It was also extremely costly. No figure has been given for the entire cost, since some of this would have come under SNCF budgets, but the first two central links cost 2,850 milliard francs. It was also consistently over budget, not only for the construction of the central link but also for conversion of the suburban lines. In the case of the Vincennes line, this shortfall was of the order of 78%. There were times when some politicians would willingly have called a halt and the project was certainly in danger in 1970/71. Fortunately the doubters did not get their way but the slowing down of development was a source of frustration to the technical staff and to the travelling public.

However, once line A was open throughout, the enthusiasm of the public for the new line was ample vindication of those who had supported its construction. In fact success soon began to bring problems of overcrowding. The Saint-Germain and Vincennes lines had together been carrying over 50 million passengers in the mid-1960s, mostly on the former, and it had been expected that the new services and the 'sparks' effect on the latter would lead to some

When line A was extended to Cergy le Haut in 1994, a new station was also provided at Nouvelle Université. Despite being in the suburbs, both lifts and escalators are provided, seen in the background. *Brian Hardy*

Success against the odds. One of the RATP's iniatives in improving the over-saturated conditions on line A was to purchase some double-deck stock. A total of 17 five-car sets entered service during 1997 and 1998. One such train is seen arriving at Torcy (in the eastern suburbs) on its journey across Paris to Cergy – Saint Christophe (in the north-west). *Brian Hardy*

increase in numbers. Even so, RATP was surprised that in 1978, the first year of complete operation, 119 million passengers were carried and by 1984 this figure had jumped to 180 million. By 1988, the section between Auber and Châtelet was carrying 54,000 passengers per hour in the morning peak, as against a planned level of 44,000. To try to cope with this, headway was reduced to one of 2.5 minutes, but operation at this density brought considerable problems if there was the slightest hitch and station dwell times were extended to unacceptable lengths. The MS61 stock began to show signs of premature ageing and in the winter of 1984/85, 38% of the fleet was out of action at any one time. Services were maintained only by the expedient of transferring some MI79 stock from line B, this in turn being made possible only by retaining the Z stock in service for longer than originally planned.

To meet this situation, RATP devised a five-point plan. Sixty-three units of a new design, MI84, were ordered, while half of the MS61 trains were given an extra-thorough overhaul. Signalling was to be revolutionised by the introduction of SACEM (*q.v.*). Experiments began with double-deck trailers, leading to the later introduction of double-deck stock. Finally, instead of using the tracks of line A between Gare de Lyon and Châtelet, line D was given separate tunnels.

THE SCEAUX LINE BECOMES LINE B

The pre-war plans for a regional network had envisaged the extension of the Sceaux line to the right bank of the Seine. However, the first plans of the 1960s ignored it completely in favour of two totally new transversal lines. One of these would have run from Roissy in the north to Evry in the south via Gare du Nord, Gare de Lyon and Gare d'Austerlitz. The second, already mentioned, would connect Cergy with Saint-Quentin-en-Yvelines via Saint-Lazare and Concorde. For the most part, these lines would require totally new construction and the only significant use of existing tracks would be in the north. The main aim of these planned lines was to serve the new towns mentioned above.

However, in 1969, the government, alarmed by the cost of line A, held an enquiry into these plans and as a result it was decided to serve the new towns, as far as possible, by diverting or extending existing lines and by utilising the Sceaux line as a single cross-river link, though the extension of Métro line 13 and its linking with line 14 went some way towards providing another cross-river facility.

Authority was given in 1972 and work began in 1973. Despite the forethought of the planners of the 1890s, it was not in fact possible to use the existing layout at Luxembourg as a starting point for the extension, since that would have required an impossibly steep gradient to bring the line below the level of the Seine. It was first necessary to lower the level of the tracks in the terminus and the sidings beyond it and while that was being done, trains terminated, not without difficulty, at Port Royal. Even with these modifications, there was still a gradient of 40.8% between Luxembourg and the cross-river tunnels. The rest of the work, though difficult, was carried out without any major problems and was completed in 1976. The unique signalling system was modified in 1977 and, after a transition period of four years, was converted to SNCF standard in 1981. The extension was opened on the same date as those of line A in December 1977. The line then became line B.

Authorisation of the extension onward to Gare du Nord had already been obtained in February of that year and work began immediately after the opening to Châtelet. This was the first time the idea of interconnexion had been put into practice, since RATP was responsible for the building of the tunnels while SNCF had already undertaken the construction of the underground station at Nord and the associated works to allow trains of line B to gain access to its suburban lines. Construction of the tunnel was complicated by the difficult nature of the subsoil of Paris in this area and the line therefore descends steeply after leaving Châtelet and climbs equally steeply on the approach to Gare du Nord, where it cut into the former terminal loop of line 5. Trains on line B arrived at Nord on 10 December 1981 where for the time being they terminated, not enough dual-voltage stock being available. From Gare du Nord, line B took over services on two lines, to Mitry and to Roissy which had already been using the underground terminus. Through trains on to these lines were instituted on 7 June 1983, by which date sufficient trains of class MI79 had been delivered. In 1988 a new station was opened at Saint-Michel giving interchange with lines 4 and 10 of the Métro as well as line C of the RER. The airport branch was extended to connect with the TGV at Roissy in a new station located under terminal two of the airport, the former, not especially convenient terminus becoming Aéroport Charles de Gaulle 1. This extension opened for traffic on 13 November 1994 and has greatly increased usage of line B by air passengers.

A platform view of Saint-Michel – Notre Dame, the only 'tube' station on the RER. *Brian Hardy*

A train of MI79 stock stands at Roissy Aéroport – Charles de Gaulle 2 on 14 September 1995. *Brian Hardy*

ORLYVAL

Now closely associated with line B is the VAL line which links Antony station to Orly airport.

In 1987 it was decided to build a completely automatic line between that station and the two terminals at the airport. The project was undertaken by the firms of Matra, who have constructed similar lines in Lille and Toulouse. It was financed entirely by the private sector and the brand name of 'OrlyVal' was chosen for it.

The 7.3km line runs partly underground for some distance from Antony, where arrival and departure platforms are on separate levels. It then comes to the surface and climbs to an elevated viaduct in the airport grounds. From Antony to Terminal Ouest trains run of the left but for the last stretch from there to Terminal Sud they observe right had running. This arrangement allows separation at Terminal Ouest of passengers for Terminal Sud from those travelling to Antony. Separate platforms at Terminal Sud keep passenger flows similarly segregated.

The rolling stock comprises eight two-coach trains. All coaches are motored and are identical to those in use in Lille. They run on rubber tyres and there are no staff on board. Each train accommodates 60 seated and 56 standing passengers, is 26.24m long and 2.06 metres wide. Maximum speed is 50km/hr. The vehicles are numbered in pairs PO1–HO1 to PO8–HO8.

The line was opened under private operation on 2 October 1991. Relatively high fares were charged and traffic levels were poor. On 4 February 1993 the line was transferred to RATP control, following which an extensive marketing campaign was undertaken. Passenger numbers have since increased considerably.

An OrlyVal train displays its new RATP livery at Orly in 1994. *RATP*

LINE C – PUTTING THE JIGSAW TOGETHER

Although a proposal to join the two somewhat cramped termini of Invalides and Quai d'Orsay had figured in the original plans of Langevin, the idea appeared to have been dropped in the immediate post-war years and did not surface again until the 1960s. While it would not have the impact of the other lines of the RER, such an extension would have the merit of avoiding reversal of trains in central Paris and would also offer interchange with the Métro at various points. Finally on 22 January 1975, the government agreed to the construction of the link and work began immediately. Re-electrification of the line from Invalides to Versailles (RG) at 1500V dc was also part of the plan and was in fact the first part of the scheme to be completed, on 27 May 1979. Tho link through to Quai d'Orsay was opened just four months later, on 30 September.

The line is worked entirely by SNCF and at first Métro tickets were not valid on the urban section, a situation which caused more than a little irritation until it was reversed in 1981. There was an imbalance of traffic between the lines to the south east, with 24 trains per hour in the evening peak, and that to Versailles, which had only eight. Some trains were therefore turned back at either Invalides or Boulevard Victor. As there were also some all-stations trains as well as semi-directs, it was all somewhat confusing compared to line A and to help passengers identify their train, a system of headcodes was devised. The first letter indicated the destination, the second the type of train and the last two letters are there simply to form an acronym. In May 1980 service was extended to Saint-Quentin-en-Yvelines and thereafter a much better balance of traffic was possible and passengers began to take to the new link with enthusiasm. Trains then operated from Étampes, Masssy, Dourdan and Orly to Versailles, Saint-Quentin or Boulevard Victor. Air passengers from Orly airport also began to make use of the line in increasing numbers.

However in 1977 it had been proposed that line C should be greatly extended as part of the Vallée de Montmorency – Invalides scheme (VMI). This would improve transport facilities in the north west of Paris and also allow an even better balance of traffic between the two ends of the line. It would also solve the by now pressing problem of modernisation of the Auteuil line, allow the ending of diesel working on the Saint-Ouen line and provide some relief to both Nord and Saint-Lazare. However, like most solutions based on use of existing facilities, the scheme also had some drawbacks.

From a new flying junction at Champ-de-Mars, trains would use the Boulainvilliers chord to reach the Auteuil line itself just south of Avenue Henri Martin. The tracks of that line would be used to a point south of Pereire, where trains would run on to the tracks of the Petite Ceinture for a short distance to Pont Berthier. From there a short section of new construction would bring them on to the Saint-Ouen line of the Nord, which would take them to Ermont-Eaubonne. From that station, trains would serve alternately Argenteuil and Montigny-Beauchamp.

There were very considerable planning difficulties and work did not begin until 1985. The new junction at Champ-de-Mars had to be constructed without interruption to the existing service and, being in cutting, posed some problems. As the bridge over the Seine had not been used by passenger trains for over sixty years, it required some rehabilitation. The Auteuil line was closed to traffic on 7 January 1985 and de-electrified prior to relaying the track and re-electrifying it at 1500V dc. Existing stations were carefully adapted to their new role. Those at Avenue Président Kennedy (formerly Passy) and Boulainvilliers were completely reconstructed and the platforms lengthened. Pressure from groups representing local inhabitants – who seem not to have noticed the rumbling of the Standard stock for over sixty years – obliged SNCF to roof over the line for much of its course. Similar 'environmental' pressure from the local council of Saint-Ouen ensured that most of the new section would have to be built in tunnel. The roof of these tunnels is used in some places to provide additional car parking space and it may be questioned just how environmentally friendly the whole action was. Terminal sidings were installed at Henri Martin and Pereire to permit short workings. The Saint-Ouen line was electrified at 25 kV ac, the change over point being located just north of the station of that name. A new station was built at Porte de Clichy to allow interchange with line 13 of the urban system. Unfortunately the planning problems referred to above meant that both this station and the reconstructed one at Saint-Ouen had to be located in a hollow and approached by gradients of 40%. The problems this has posed for trains entering and leaving these stations can well be imagined! Construction of Porte de Clichy proved exceptionally difficult and the station was not opened until September 1991. Gennevilliers may in future provide interchange with an extension of tram line T1. All works, with the exception mentioned above, were completed in 1988 and service began on 25 September that year, considerably later than had originally been expected. The extension cost 1,065 million francs at 1981 prices and was expected to bring a 33% cost-benefit rate of return.

There is no doubt that the extension, serving a dormitory area with a population of almost one million, has been a success, not only in relieving the main line termini in the manner expected but also saving around 4,000 car journeys each day. Interchange facilities with nine lines of the urban system are excellent, although the new line has brought additional traffic on to the already-overloaded branch of line 13 and this problem will not finally be solved until that is connected to an extended line 14. The journey over the former Auteuil line is somewhat tedious, being almost entirely in tunnel, and local passengers have been deprived of the frequent service formerly provided by its trains and the connexion to Saint-Lazare. For those travelling longer distances, the route is somewhat circuitous and anyone wanting to go from Saint-Michel to Ermont as quickly as possible would probably still do better to go to Gare du Nord by line B and proceed by suburban train, if prepared to brave the crowds at Nord. But of course a direct service offers a more convenient journey. The extension of line C has been a sometimes uneasy compromise between the needs of different groups of passengers. A further extension to Pontoise opened on 28 August 2000.

A class Z8800 at Avenue Président Kennedy on 25 December 1991. Both RER and Métro operate a normal Sunday service on Christmas Day.
Brian Hardy

A platform view of the reopened Boulainvilliers station, seen on 6 May 1994.
Brian Hardy

The original tiled name at Boulainvilliers has been carefully restored.
Brian Hardy

LINE D - INTERCONNEXION IN PRACTICE

Unlike all earlier RER lines, line D did not require any construction work outside the central area of Paris. Approval in principle for the scheme was originally given by the Syndicat des Transports Parisiens in 1976. However, service on the line did not begin until 27 September 1987 when trains from Villiers-le-Bel were diverted at Gare du Nord into the underground station and so on to Châtelet, using the tracks of line B. There was now easy interchange for passengers from that part of the northern suburbs to line A and this facility no doubt helped to increase the overloading of its central portion. On 28 January 1990 trains serving Goussainville and Orry-la-Ville were similarly extended.

On 27 June 1988 there was a serious collision between two trains in the underground suburban station at Gare de Lyon in which 59 people were killed and 32 seriously injured. These are today remembered by a memorial in the station. Following this incident, members of the National Assembly began to campaign for a start to be made on the new tunnels for line D, on the slightly tenuous grounds that the accident would not have occurred if Gare de Lyon had been a through underground station. In the early months of 1990 the STP agreed to the construction of the new line and work began at Gare de Lyon in the autumn of 1991. Work on the other three sections began in 1992.

Line D serves the central tracks at Châtelet – Les Halles. On leaving that station, the three tracks merge into two, passing under the tunnels of lines 1, 4 and 11, lying beside those of line A and passing under the southbound tunnel of line B. Due to the congested nature of this area, it was not possible to use a tunneling shield and all work on lot D1 was carried out from two shafts, the subsoil having been previously consolidated by a silicon jelly. From this point to the special work giving access to Gare de Lyon, the eastbound track of line D lies between the two tunnels of line A, while the westbound track lies to the south of these. They then enter two single-track tunnels, each 6.30m in diameter, and at a depth of 20m, running below a large underground car park at Hôtel de Ville. Provision for the new tunnels was made when the latter was constructed. As the subsoil in this area is hard, excavation was done by a shield operating from two shafts. Lot D2 ran as far as Boulevard de la Bastille. Just before this point, the tunnels pass below those of line 5 to join the part already prepared as lot D3, leading on to Boulevard Diderot. Here the two tunnels converge into one of 11.70m diameter in which is situated the special work giving access to Gare de Lyon underground station. Immediately south of this tunnel is that for line 14, which was excavated at the same time to minimise disruption. Work on this section as also carried out entirely underground, using prefabricated beams to support the roof. Finally lot D4 linked this section to the station, passing under the chord linking lines 1 and 5. As this section was excavated in the open air, great care had to be taken to keep disruption to the traffic to a minimum. The space between the new tunnels and the surface is filled by a three-storey underground car park.

It was certainly no mean achievement to construct 2.5km of new tunnels through an area filled on the surface with buildings of architectural and historic interest and below ground with an existing network of tunnels both for rail services and the various other utilities. The cost, at 1989 prices, was estimated to be 1,300 million francs, but this had risen to 1,550 by the time work was completed. Of this, 40% was a grant from the Region, 40% a grant from central government and 20% a loan from the Region.

Through services between line D and the existing services from Gare de Lyon began with the winter timetable in 1995 from 24 September, but almost immediately ran into trouble as drivers from the Nord's section had not been given sufficient training on the ex-PLM south eastern lines. Even after that problem had been dealt with, others remained and until 1998 punctuality on line D (alone on the suburban network) consistently fell below 90%. In that year, the timetable was rearranged but even so in the autumn of 1998, punctuality was still only 93.8%. Nonetheless, the new facility is of great benefit to many suburban passengers and is estimated to carry 20,000 passengers per hour on the central section in peak periods, of whom about 12,000 may previously have used line A. It also makes the change of trains in Paris much easier for long-distance passengers from north and south east.

In January 1998 a new station was opened between Gare du Nord and Saint-Denis. Known as Stade de France – Saint-Denis, it is located near the new stadium which was built to house the games for the football World Cup of 1998. It is a four track station with two island platforms, the outer faces being used by regular services and the inner by special workings. Access is by ramps and a wide avenue leads to the stadium, located 1.2km away. Together with the resited station of La Plaine – Stade de France on line B, the station preformed very well during that season and it was found that it could easily accept or deliver 25,000 passengers per hour.

Garges Sarcelles is a busy station on the northern section of line D. *Brian Hardy*

LINE E – EST–OUEST LIAISON EXPRESS

While the new towns created in the 1960s have successfully coped with the growth of population in Ile-de-France, this growth has been unbalanced and the greatest increases have occurred in the east, particularly in Marne-la-Vallée. However, the growth in employment has been concentrated in the west, particularly around La Défense and in the VIIIth and IXth arrondissements, roughly the area delineated by Etoile, Concorde and Gare du Nord. The result of this imbalance has been an unforeseen increase in commuting, manifested by the overcrowding of line A, the only RER line then serving the eastern part of the Region. Meanwhile an increase in the number of commuters using Gare de l'Est. has in turn further overloaded lines 4 and 7. It is anticipated that commuting from the eastern suburbs into Paris will increase by 30% between 2000 and 2015, while commuting from suburb to suburb will increase by 70%. These figures are the result of a very thorough origin-destination survey carried out by the Syndicat des Transports Parisiens in 1991–92 and a survey carried out in 1993 at prinicpal SNCF stations in Ile-de-France. Only a new line of the RER could respond to the demands of the situation.

Even before these surveys were carried out, the management of SNCF, aware of what was happening on or, more accurately, below the ground had proposed to the STP outline plans for a new RER line. This would take the suburban services from Chelles-Gournay and Villiers-sur-Marne together with a new branch from La Varenne-Chennevières to a terminus somewhere in the VIIIth or IXth arrondissements via a new tunnel with stations at Magenta, between Gare du Nord and Gare de l'Est, and Condorcet, beside Saint-Lazare. This would relieve line A, to which many eastern passengers transferred at Val-de-Fontenay, the Métro lines serving the two termini and several busy bus lines.

The Syndicat approved the plans on 31 July 1990 and a declaration of public utility followed on 15 November 1991, ministerial approval being obtained just one week later. The proposed new branch was, however, cut back to Plant-le-Champigny. For what was now spoken of as the first stage, Condorcet would be the terminus. In 1998 it was decided that this station would in fact be called Haussmann – Saint-Lazare. The new line would provide interchange with lines B, D, 2, 4, 5 and 7 at Magenta and lines A, 3, 9, 12, 13 and later 14 at its terminus. It was estimated that line A would be relieved of about 8,000 passengers per hour between Auber and Gare de Lyon, while 10,500 passengers would no longer have to use lines 4 and 7 in the peak periods. Overall, a cost-benefit return of around 21% was expected, while the journeys of around 77 million passengers per annum would be significantly improved. In both the new terminal stations, careful attention to passenger flow would ensure that the large numbers of passengers entering or leaving did not cause congestion above ground and that these flows would be diffused over a wide area.

It was not assumed that it would be easy to insert another new line through the complex geology and urban geography of Paris, but in the event, the difficulties were greater than had been foreseen. The acquisition of property to be demolished took three years and required a considerable sum of money. The formula used to calculate such payments was first devised thirty years previously, for use when line A was being built, at a time when much less regard was paid to environmental considerations. Many of those affected now contested the calculations and the cost rose to 600 million francs. There were also problems with buildings which had to be underpinned or whose façade had to be preserved.

This view of the station at Rosny Bois-Perrier in July 1999 shows the reconstruction works undertaken at suburban stations in connexion with conversion to RER operation. Even although the inauguration of service on the branch to Villiers-sur-Marne was only days away, a good deal remained to be done! In the background, an elderly electric locomotive, still in its original green livery, has a train of RIB stock, soon to be replaced by the new double-deck multiple units.
Brian Patton

The geology was also complex. The new tunnel descends for most of its length before rising slightly as it approaches Haussmann and in doing so passes through a layer of sandstone then a layer of limestone interspersed with projections of gypsum. From Magenta onwards, the subsoil is also very wet. A preliminary survey to assess the best means of dealing with the subsoil lasted from June 1990 to February 1992 and also examined and mapped the location of disused pipes and other public utilities.

Using the information thus gathered, it was decided that, as far as possible, the shafts to be used as future emergency exits should be used as working shafts and that the débris from the tunnelling operations should be removed underground, to a site on SNCF land adjacent to Gare de l'Est. Simply to open up an enormous hole, as was done in the 1970s, was no longer acceptable!

The first section, which was on these railway lands, was excavated by cut and cover methods, while the second part to Magenta was worked by traditional methods. From that station onwards, a shield was used. Single track tunnels are either 5.80m or 6.40m in diameter and double track tunnels are 9.40m in diameter. Stations are 225m long, 58m wide with a vault of 21.2m, to allow for four platform faces. The sheer extent of the excavation required for each of these – and both are in particularly waterlogged areas – made it essential to find a method of stabilising the works as soon as possible after completion. This was achieved by the Jacobson method, by which the supports for the vault are pushed upwards into position as soon as the preliminary excavation has been made, to give supporting arcs and allow the finishing work to be carried out at a more relaxed pace.

The works for line E have not been confined to tunnelling and tunnel sections. Connexions to existing lines by ramps had to be made north of Gare de l'Est. A flying junction had therefore to be constructed at Pantin and the junction at Noisy-le-Sec had to be reorganised. A new substation had to be built in the same area and existing substations upgraded to allow them to cope with the increased loadings. A new signalling system was installed to control the signals in the tunnels and on surface as far as Noisy-le-Sec. Details of the rebuilding of the depot at that location are given in the chapter on depots. At most stations platform height had to be increased and canopies lengthened and, to allow one-person operation, closed circuit television was installed. Finally, all telecommunications had to be upgraded for the new service, to allow an improved passenger information system to be used. This system, known as Infogare, provides real time information on the next six trains to pass through a station and is installed not only on platforms but at locations such as the top of escalators leading to platforms. A somewhat similar system, Infotrain, allows on-board transmission of information to passengers both visually, by liquid crystal displays on monitors, and aurally. It may also be used for publicity purposes. The total cost of all those works was 1,850 million francs.

For the first time, 25kV ac has been used in a tunnel section through the central area of Paris, all previous schemes having used 1500V dc. Maximum speed over this section is 80km/hr.

The first optimistic assumptions were that the new line would be ready in 1998, but the difficulties with property outlined above caused a revision of the opening date and the first train to use the new line was a test train on 22 July 1998. This consisted of a set of Z22500 stock and was pushed by a diesel locomotive as far as Magenta. It was not until Bastille Day (14 July) 1999 that public service began, two days after the line was officially opened by Prime Minister Lionel Jospin. On that occasion, two trains, made up of sets carrying the inaugural livery, ran in parallel through the tunnel to Haussmann. Unlike M Giscard d'Estaing, M Jospin did not try his hand at driving! Service was initially provided only to Chelles-Gournay, that on the branch to Villiers-sur-Marne being opened on 30 August 1999. Service to Le Plant-Champigny will follow at a later date in 2000.

Four trains per hour provide off-peak service on each branch, in itself a considerable improvement on what was formerly offered. In peak periods, there will be four trains every quarter hour, two to and from Chelles and one each on the other two branches. As all of these will call at Val-de-Fontenay, it is hoped that a considerable number of passengers will now transfer from line A, rather than on to it as was formerly the case. A shuttle service of two trains per hour between Magenta and Haussmann operated from 14 July to 30 August 1999 and this could be revived if demand increases.

The use of Haussmann as a terminus was intended to be only temporary, since it will inevitably limit the number of trains which can use the new link to 16 per direction per hour. It was originally stated that the long-term plan was that line should be extended in tunnel to Pont Cardinet, where it would pick up the services to Versailles (RD) and Saint-Nom-la-Bretèche. Such an extension would virtually double the capacity of the line and also allow the construction of a new station north of Gare de l'Est at Evangile-Aubervilliers, in an area with relatively poor public transport links. This station would also improve access to the Cité des Sciences de La Villette. It would then theoretically be possible to run 32 trains per hour per direction through the tunnels, although initially at least, the number would probably be 20. It was envisaged that the line would be worked in two groups of services which would overlap in the central area. Those from the west would run to Noisy-le-Sec while those from the east would terminate at Pont Cardinet. The new line could, alternatively, run to the east of Saint-Lazare, to allow interchange with line C and line 13 at Porte de Clichy. This course would also allow construction to take place on railway-owned land and would cause less interruption to existing services out of Saint-Lazare.

Unfortunately the considerable over-spend on the new line appears to have postponed any decision on the further extension and no date has been set for a resumption of work west of Haussmann. The above mentioned plans must therefore be considered subject to change at a later date and it is unlikely that any such extension will be open before 2010. It would be a pity if line E is confined to the section open at present and not allowed to realise its full potential.

The two units of class Z22500 used for the official inauguration of line E on 14 July 1999 were decorated with a map of the line. One of these sets is seen later in the same month at Chelles-Gournay. *Brian Patton*

Having reversed at Chelles-Gournay, a set of class Z22500 re-enters the station prior to returning to Haussmann – Saint-Lazare in July 1999. *Brian Patton*

Given the results of the various surveys mentioned above, it is likely that future expansion of the rail system in Ile-de-France will be in the outer areas and that new projects within Paris and the inner suburbs will take the form of light rail and some additional Métro extensions, rather than large scale projects on the RER.

To improve inter-suburban links, and decrease car use in peak periods, two new tangential lines will be brought into operation. The north tangential line will run from Sartrouville to Noisy-le-Sec, with a possible branch to Roissy. The west and south tangential line will run from Versailles to Massy and Corbeil. Both of these lines will make use of much existing track, especially that of the Grande Ceinture, and as a result will cost in the region of 60 million francs per kilometre, about one sixth of the cost of one kilometre of line E within Paris. About 80% of the rail network of Ile-de-France will then serve 75% of its population, either directly or by interchange. The schemes fit in well with the ideas outlined in the Schéma Directeur of 1994 and in late 1999 were adopted as part of the next stage of the seven year plan under it. If approved by the STP, a declaration of public utility will be requested in 2001, with the aim of bringing the lines into operation in 2005. Rolling stock envisaged would be class Z23500, as used on services in the provinces, but with three coaches instead of two. There will be a basic quarter hourly service at peak periods and a half hourly service at other times. Although not worked as part of the RER, these lines would offer interchange facilities at many points on RER lines. This scheme has been named Lutèce, a form of the Roman name for Paris.

Another possible new line will be one linking Ermont-Eaubonne direct with Saint-Lazare. A link in tunnel via Quai d'Orsay to Montparnasse, with connexion to its suburban services to Rambouillet and Plaisir-Grignon, may follow at a later date. This would function as RER line F and would have interchange with line C and the extended line E. It would be the last such link within Paris. There would be stations at Pont Cardinet, Saint-Lazare, Musée d'Orsay and Montparnasse. However, it is unlikely that any action will be taken on this link before 2010.

On the other hand, the heavy rail service on the line from Bondy to Aulnay-sous-Bois will be converted to light rail, with a link at Noisy to the extended line T1 and a tram link might also be provided between Saint-Germain RER and Saint-Germain – Grande Ceinture.

Existing RER lines may be extended as follows:

Line A beyond Cergy towards Mantes;
Line B from Roissy to Damartin;
Line C to Pontoise and La Verrière;
Line D from Corbeil to Senart;
Line E from Chelles-Gournay to Meaux and/or to Marne-la-Vallèe and Sucy-en-Brie and from Villiers to Tournan;
The service from La Défense to Saint-Quentin-en-Yvelines may be extended to Rambouillet.

There is no timetable for these extensions, although all have been adopted under the Schéma Directeur of 1994.

The equivalent plan for the inner area is named Orbitale. Under it, plans for the next seven years envisage the following tramway extensions:

Extension of line T1 from Bobigny to Noisy-le-Sec (already under construction) and on to Val-de-Fontenay, and from Saint-Denis to Epinay-Villetaneuse Extension of line T2 from Issy Val-de-Seine to Porte de Versailles and from La Défense to Colombes and Bezons;

New tram lines from Villejuif to Juvisy, from Châtillon to Viroflay and from Porte de Versailles to Porte d'Ivry.

Of the extensions to the Métro mentioned in the handbook on that system, the following have now been adopted:

Line 4 from Porte d'Orléans to Mairie de Montrouge (1.5km);
Line 8 from Créteil Préfecture to Créteil Sud (1.2km);
Line 12 from Porte de la Chapelle to Pont de Stains (2.3km);
Line 13 from Gabriel Péri to Gennevilliers and Le Luth (1.8km);
Line 14 from Madeleine to Saint-Lazarre (600m) and from Bibliothèque to Olympiades (1.7km).

The indicator on the westbound platform at Noisiel, showing the departure times of the next three trains, all bound for Cergy, July 2000. *Brian Patton*

SERVICE PATTERNS

The destination indicator at Cergy le Haut in January 1995 displays headcode, departure time, train length (long/short) and stations served.
Brian Hardy

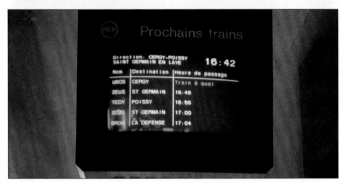

Many RER station platforms have screens which indicate the next five trains and the predicted times of arrival. This one is on the westbound platform at Charles de Gaulle – Etoile on line A.
Brian Hardy

The complete service pattern of all RER services is complicated and a detailed list of all possible permutations would require a complete book of its own. A summary of the basic daytime off-peak service for each line is given here. No major changes to this pattern are expected within the next few years, but there could be minor modifications. It should be noted that during the summer holiday period, which runs generally from late July until the end of August, the pattern is often quite different. Readers who require a more detailed record or additional information are recommended to consult the Indicateur Horaires which are published for each line by SNCF and, in addition to complete timetables, give a list of all headcodes and much other useful service information. These booklets are inexpensive, the price in 2000 being 11 francs per volume.

LINE A. Basic service of four trains per 20 minutes:

West to East

2 Saint-Germain – Boissy-Saint-Léger, all stations.	Code NEGE
1 Poissy – Torcy, all stations	Code OKEY
1 Cergy – Marne-la-Vallée, all stations	Code QYAN

East to West

The above service operates in the reverse direction, codes ZEBU, UBOS and TEDY respectively.

LINE B. Basic service of three trains per quarter hour:

North to South
1 Aéroport CDG2 – Massy-Palaiseau, non-stop CDG1 – Gare du Nord,
then all stations.   Code KROL
1 Aeroport CDG2 – Saint-Rémy-lès-Chevreuse, all stations to Cité Universitaire, then Bourg-la-Reine, Antony, Massy-Palaiseau, then all stations.
                                                                     Code PEPE
1 Mitry-Claye – Robinson, all stations except Blanc-Mesnil, Drancy,
Courneuve-Aubervilliers and La Plaine-Stade de France.   Code SPAC

South to North
The above service operates in the reverse direction, with codes EKLI, EFLA and
ICAR respectively.

It should be noted that on lines A and B, the headcodes are combined with a
two digit running number, using even numbers westbound and soutbound
respectively and odd numbers eastbound and northbound respectively. When
these numbers reach 98/99, the last two letters of the headcode change for the
remainder of the day, the first two letters remaining the same.

LINE C. The service is six trains per half hour:

West/North to East/South
1 Saint-Quentin-en-Yvelines – Saint-Martin d'Etampes, all stations to
Austerlitz, Juvisy, Brétigny, all stations to Saint-Martin and all stations
to Dourdan.   Code YETI
1 Argenteuil – all stations to Pont de Rungis.   Code ROMA
1 Montigny-Beauchamp – all stations to Massy-Palaiseau.
                                                                     Code MONA
1 Versailles CH – all stations to Versailles RG via Massy-Palaiseau and
Juvisy.   Code VICK
1 Viroflay RG – all stations to Austerlitz – Choisy-le-Roi, all stations to
Savigny-sur-Orge.   Code CIME
1 Invalides – all stations to Austerlitz – Juvisy – all stations to Brétigny.
                                                                     Code BALI

The same service operates in the reverse direction. Codes are SLIM, GOTA,
NORA, CIME, VICK and LARA.

LINE D. The basic service is one of three trains per half hour.

North to South
1 Villiers-le-Bel, all stations to Gare de Lyon, Villeneuve-Saint-Georges,
Melun.   Code ZYCK
1 Orry-la-Ville, all stations to Villiers-le-Bel, Gare du Nord, all stations to
Corbeil via Evry.   Code RIPE.
1 Villiers-le-Bel, all stations to Corbeil via Evry.   Code ZOVE.

South to North
The same service operates in reverse. Codes are VICK, VOPE and HAVU.

LINE E

The basic service is one of four trains per half hour, each branch alternately.
Codes COLE (Chelles) or VALO (Villiers) outbound, HOLE and HALO, inbound.

STOCK NO LONGER IN SERVICE

THE Z STOCK

To provide electric service on the Sceaux line, the CMP took delivery of what has always been known as the Z stock. In fact, the letter Z is used by SNCF as the code letter for any electric motor coach and all present-day RER stock belonging to SNCF is Z stock. Perhaps the class under review should be referred to as 'the' Z stock.

This class was designed from new by CMP staff, since existing suburban electric stock could not offer the standards of performance which would be expected on the line. The design was based closely on that of the trains most recently built for the Métro, but, to obtain maximum flexibility, all coaches were motored, with a single driving cab. A first order for 57 coaches for the CMP was placed on 16 January 1934 and a supplementary order was later placed for four additional coaches plus 14 for the PO company, these not actually being delivered until after the formation of SNCF. Further batches were ordered as detailed in the table at the end of this section. Apart from the rounded lower corners in the windows of the last delivery, all were externally identical. The SNCF coaches became part of the RATP fleet in 1964.

Z stock coach Z23329 leads an eight-coach train into Saint-Rémy-Lès-Chevreuse on 24 September 1984. *Brian Hardy*

All-metal construction was used and the Z class were handsome vehicles, with domed roofs, wide windows and four double doors on each side, each of these having a clear opening of 1m. The driving cabs were half width and it was possible for crews to move through a train by inter-communicating doors. To assist both passengers and staff to identify a train, a three-digit headcode was fitted. Automatic Willison couplers allowed rapid reformation of trains according to traffic needs.

Each coach had 16 seats in first class and 40 in second, plus 8 and 21 respectively on 'strapontins' or tip-up seats in the vestibules. There was officially room for 30 standing passengers in first and 91 in second but, especially in war time, these figures were often exceeded. The first class sections were at the inner end of each coach and were thus normally adjacent in service.

Internally the coaches were a vast improvement in comfort over the steam-hauled stock which they replaced. The seats had backs of medium height and were covered in chestnut-coloured synthetic leather in second class and patterned grey-pink velour in first. There was a generous amount of leg room between seats. Roof mounted ventilators provided a comfortable environment, even with all windows closed, and were complemented, in all but the last two series, by light fittings of classic Art Deco style. The last two batches had fluorescent lighting from new and formica panelling was fitted in place of the stove enamel of earlier sets. Pennsylvania bogies gave a smooth ride.

An interior view of a coach of Z stock, showing the decorative panelling of the earlier batches of this class. *Brian Hardy*

A comparable view of a later member of the class with plain panelling. *Brian Hardy*

Each coach had two Jeumont TC127 motors of 174kW mounted on one bogie, giving a top speed of 80km/hr. Control was by a servo motor with 16 contactors, mounted under the body. Air brakes alone were provided. An audible and visual automatic warning system was fitted in the driving cab and duplicated at the guard's post, the latter being able to take over in the event of anything happening to the driver. A chrono-tachograph, similar to the flight recorder of an aircraft, noted speeds, times and observance of signals. Overall length was 20.6m, width 3.2m and unladen weight was 44.6 tonnes.

The Z stock proved to be successful in service and much livelier than the Standard stock of the Ouest. The design having been well thought-out, there were few modifications during quite a long career. When six-coach formations were introduced in 1961, the original pneumatic door control was replaced by electro-pneumatic equipment. This also allowed the later expansion to eight-coach trains in 1980. In the 1970s, fluorescent lighting replaced the Art Deco fixtures of the earlier batches. The most substantial alteration was that made to 55 coaches which were converted to one-person operation in 1976. This involved the fitting of an automatic safety system and the repositioning of the door closure control into the driving cab. Thereafter, unmodified coaches, like the 'Passviertel' trains on the Berlin S-Bahn, could not operate at the end of a train and had the number boxes blanked off. In preparation for incorporation into the RER and the extension to Châtelet, a public address system was fitted to Z stock in 1977. As there was some concern about the ability of the braking system of the class to cope with the descent of 40.8mm/m encountered by north-bound trains on leaving Luxembourg, trials were conducted with several units in June 1976 on the gradient between Le Pecq and Saint-Germain on line A. Following these, alterations were made to the air brakes, the triple valve system being replaced by a Westinghouse system. Monobloc wheels were fitted to prevent any melting of tyres with the heat generated.

The Z stock was originally painted duck-egg blue, with a white roof, the doors and windows of the first class section being outlined in red. The roofs were painted dark grey during the war and the attractive but slightly impractical livery gave way after 1946 to standard, dreary SNCF green with black roof. When incorporated into the RER, the stock was repainted in to that system's light blue and grey, with a dark grey roof.

Apart from two coaches which were victims of Allied bombing at Massy-Palaiseau in June 1944, the class remained intact until 1982. From 1984, withdrawals were rapid, although the problems of line A gave some members of the class an extended lease of life. The last Z train ran on 27 February 1987 and was given a send-off on 19 September 1987 almost equal to that given to the Sprague stock of the Métro four years previously.

No fewer than 14 coaches survive, six having been kept by RATP and eight purchased privately. An example, with its original number of Z23461 replaced – it was one of the PO batch – was carefully restored to pristine condition by the RATP workshop staff at Montrouge. During its working life of 46 years, it clocked up 2,924,762km in service. The original triple-valve braking system was replaced from stock items, but other parts had to be made new. The fluorescent tubes were removed and classic lamp holders replaced, but these are made of translucent resin rather than glass, A floor covering of epoxy resin closely resembles the original magnesium cement. The upholsterers at Fontenay works were able to recreate the original design used on the seats in first class from a tiny fragment of cloth which had been saved. The door controls were also replaced by the original design and line diagrams and signs were recreated from photographs. One of the greatest problems was the recreation of the original livery, but careful study of photographs and models led to an excellent result. This beautifully restored coach makes an excellent addition to the national railway museum. A second, ex-CMP coach has been preserved in the Musée de l'Ile de France at Sceaux.

Numbering and construction of Z stock, with dates of ordering and entry to service are as follows:

CMP STOCK

Z23221–23241	Établissements Decauville	1934	1937
Z23242–23265	Cie Francaise de Matériel de C de Fer	1934	1937
Z23266–23277	Cie Générale des Constructions	1934	1937
Z23278–23281	Cie Francaise de Matériel de C de Fer	1937	1938
Z23282–23296	Brissoneau et Lotz	1942	1947
Z23297–23310	CIMT	1950	1952
Z23311–23331	CIMT	1959	1961
Z23332–23356	CIMT	1961	1962

Z23234 and Z23241 were destroyed in an air raid in June 1944

Z23282–23290 and Z23311–23356 were modified for one-person operation.

PO/SNCF STOCK

Z23451–23464	Cie Francaise de Matériel de C de Fer	1937	1938

These were renumbered Z3401–3414 in 1940 and further renumbered to Z23401–23414 on acquisition by RATP in 1964.

The farewell trip of the Z stock on 19 September 1987 drew considerable crowds. This is the scene at Massy-Palaiseau. *Brian Hardy*

RER STOCK IN SERVICE IN YEAR 2000 – SNCF

CLASS Z5300

The first stock to work on line C was of typical SNCF design for suburban stock of the period 1950–1975. Class Z5300 had first entered service in 1965 and was based closely on the three-coach class Z5100, which had been placed in service on the newly electrified lines out of the Gare de Lyon in 1954 and which was in turn based on the very successful class Z23700 introduced by the État in 1937. Like that stock, class Z5300 has stainless steel bodywork. The new stock was made up into four-coach sets, consisting of a second class driving motor with guard's space, two second class trailers and a composite control trailer. In service, up to three sets can be coupled together. In all, 145 sets were delivered between 1965 and 1975, of which 71, all from the later deliveries, are used on line C. These sets, and a few used elsewhere, have gangways between coaches, for use by staff only, but are not gangwayed between sets. For use on line C, they were fitted with number panels above the windscreen of the driving cab. The motor coach and one trailer have toilet accommodation.

Unit Z5397 of class Z5300 heads a Versailles CH – Versailles RG train off the Grande Ceinture line into Massy-Palaiseau in March 1997. *Brian Patton*

The class was built by Carel et Fouché, who had secured from the Budd company the European patents for this form of construction. Oerlikon electrical equipment is fitted. Total seating capacity is 469. Seating, in orange pvc, was 3+2 in second class and 2+2 in first, but, as common on SNCF suburban stock, was of the same type throughout. The original bench type sets have, however, been replaced by seats of individual configuration.

There are three double doors per side on each coach. These are slightly angled and have to be operated manually once released by the guard and, as they are rather heavy, this is not an easy task for an elderly passenger on a low platform.

Four 245kW motors give a top service speed of 120km/hr, although the class is now authorised to run at 140km/hr in emergency. These sets are noted for their smooth riding, but acceleration is noisy and ponderous. Total weight is 164 tonnes, of which 62 are accounted for by the motor coach, and lengths are 25.9m, 25.6m, 25.6m and 25.9m, giving an overall figure of around 115m. As it is limited to lines electrified at 1500V dc, the class is confined to those services of line C which run entirely on the left bank of the Seine and they also work the almost-circular service from Versailles (CH) to Versailles (RG) via Massy, Juvissy and Austerlitz. They can be operated to stations with either low or medium height platforms.

As the capacity and performance of this class are below that which is now considered essential for RER service, it is in course of withdrawal from line C. Displaced sets will move to Montparnasse, where they will replace RIB locomotive hauled stock. For this reason, it has not been converted for one-person operation, nor can passengers communicate with the driver. When running with the motor coach leading, guards normally travel in the driver's cab. Door control switches and the signal bell are located above the leading doorway.

The sets used on RER service are numbered as follows:

    5373   25446   25445   15373

in sequence to

    5445   25590   25589   15445

Car 5395 carries the name ISSY-LES-MOULINEAUX

The RER sets are shedded at Paris Austerlitz.

CLASS Z5600 AND ASSOCIATED TRAILERS

In view of the deficiencies of class Z5300 and the success of double-deck loco-motive-hauled stock of class VB2N (*q.v.*), SNCF managers took the decision to apply this concept to new stock which could operate both on line C and on suburban service out of Gare de Lyon. The result was class Z5600.

This class is made up of 104 motor coaches, normally operating in married pairs. A pair with two intermediate trailers is the minimum used in service and two such sets make up peak-hour trains on line C. There are 117 second class trailers and (originally) 100 composite trailers. Trailers are used in common with class Z8800 and the composition of a set may therefore vary from time to time, but paired motor coaches are always kept together. Normally 58 four coach sets are used on line C. Motor coaches were second class only and one vehicle in each pair is fitted with a toilet. One trailer in each set was composite. Until recently the upper saloon was used for smokers but sets have now become non-smoking throughout. Seating is provided for 115 passengers per motor coach, 168 per second class trailer and 152 per composite trailer. With the use of some 'strap-ontins' (tip-up seats) in the vestibules, a four-coach set seats 580 and can also take a further 250 standing passengers, at three per square metre. Seating was again 3+2 in second class and 2+2 in first and, as with class Z5300, the first class fare bought only additional space. Given the weight and length of a train, total capacity is impressive but, as there are only two double-width doors on each side of a coach, dwell times at busy stations can be prolonged.

An interior view of the lower deck of type Z5600/8800. The brown plastic seating is typical in the 3+2 arrangement. *Brian Hardy*

Repaints of classes Z5600 and Z8800 have seen a revised scheme for the front end, in which the red colour is extended over the roof dome, previously white. One such train on line C arrives at Issy – Val-de-Seine. *Brian Hardy*

Test running with the first set began in the autumn of 1982 but the production series was built between 1983 and 1985 by Ateliers de Construction du Nord de la France, with electrical equipment by what was then simply Alsthom. Four 350kW motors per motor coach and chopper control give a much improved performance when compared with class Z5300 – though as long as the latter remains in service it is not possible to take advantage of this – and top speed is 140km/hr. Motor coaches are 25.10m long and weigh 66 tonnes, while trailers are 24.3m long and weigh 42 tonnes. The sets are equipped for driver-only operation and there is passenger–driver communication. As with class Z5300, this class is confined to 1500V dc lines. This means that on line C, they operate only services on the Left Bank of the Seine. First use on RER service was from June 1985.

The class was painted from new in the red, white and blue Ile-de-France livery, which at present it still carries. Sets used on RER service have a display panel for the letter code above the windscreen.

Motor coaches are numbered in sequence from 5601/5602 to 5703/5704. Trailer seconds are numbered from 25601 to 25717 and trailer composites are from 35601 to 35700. A few motor coaches are named, as follows:

5601/5602	SAVIGNY-LE-TEMPLE	5697/5698	BRETIGNY-SUR-ORGE
5633/5634	ARTIS-MONS	5699/5700	ETAMPES
5635/5636	VIROFLAY		

These carry an attractive badge incorporating the name and coat of arms of the community concerned.

RER sets work out of the depot of Paris Sud-Ouest. The other members of the class are based at Villeneuve and work on suburban services from Gare de Lyon. They now operate with four trailers, with a consequent slight reduction in performance.

CLASS Z8800

This is a dual-voltage version of class Z5600 and was built between 1986 and 1988 for use on the VMI services to Ermont-Eaubonne. The class consists of 58 sets of married pairs of motor coaches. As these have a transformer, they seat only 107 passengers per coach and weigh 69 tonnes. In all other respects, they are identical to their predecessors and, as stated above, share trailers with these. This class is used only on RER services. The first set arrived in 1984 and was tested extensively in the Toulon area. Series delivery began in July 1985 and at that time, a few sets were used on the northern part of the future line D from Gare du Nord. The class began to operate the VMI services of line C in the winter timetable of 1988 and is now concentrated entirely on these services. The area above the cab is painted blue rather than white and the class can be distinguished by this feature from class Z5600.

Numbers run in sequence from 8801/8802 through to 8915/8916. Names are carried as follows:

8801/8802	SAINT GRATIEN	8803/8804	FRANCONVILLE
8805/8806	GROSSLAY	8807/8808	SANNOIS
8809/8810	ERMONT-EAUBONNE	8811/8812	GENNEVILLIERS

All are shedded at Les Ardoines.

A contrast in front ends at Chaville-Vélizy on 22 July 2000. Between coaches 8805 on the left and 20511 is the large box containing the cctv to allow drivers to observe the platform. *Brian Patton*

CLASS Z20500

This class, built between 1988 and 1996, is in turn a development of class Z8800 and is also equipped for dual-voltage operation. Though built for use on line D, it may also be seen on line C.

The class also operates many other services in several different formations and similar stock is used in the Nord-Pas de Calais Region Although the class has been in service for just over ten years, its history is already fairly complex. There are 119 sets in total and details of numbering and entry to service are given in a table at the end of this section. Unlike the previous class, these trains are operated in both four and five coach formation and have trailers of two different lengths.

The class was built by the Compagnie Industrielle de Matériel de Transport and ANF and has electrical equipment by GEC-Alsthom. Trailers are slightly longer than those of class Z5600/Z8800 and as a result a four-coach set can seat 600 passengers and has a total capacity of 900. One trailer in each set has a toilet.

Electrically, class Z20500 differs in having asynchronous motors but the output and hence speed are the same as in earlier classes. Unit 20887/8 has GEC-Alsthom 'Onix' drive in place of thyristor control and during tests of this, it ran in Normandy. Motor coaches have a length of 25.1m and weigh 65 tonnes.

A unit of class Z20500 at Versailles – Chantiers in March 1997. *Brian Patton*

An upper deck view of a coach of class Z20500. *Brian Hardy*

To take maximum advantage of the loading gauge the class was constructed to a more upright and angular profile, by which it may be distinguished. This form of construction has given a more spacious internal appearance to the upper saloon and lighting has also been improved. Seats are arranged as before but the orange pvc has given way to a more subdued brown vandal-resistant fabric and interior fittings are rather more basic.

The first set, Z20501/20502, entered trial service in June 1988 and delivery of this batch was completed by March 1989. Eight went to Les Ardoines to strengthen services on line C and the balance went to Les Joncherelles, to allow the borrowed members of class Z8800 to return to line C. The trailers of this batch are 26.4m long, allowing a slight increase in capacity for an increased weight of 1.5 tonnes. A four coach train can accommodate 1064 passengers instead of 995, with seating space for 80 in first class and 520 in second.

The second batch of 21 sets entered service between June 1991 and February 1992. This delivery was divided between Villeneuve, for use on the future southern section of line D, and Les Ardoines for the new service from Saint-Quentin to La Défense. At this stage, some sets exchanged their long trailers for those of shorter length from earlier classes.

In late 1992 and 1993, Villeneuve received a further 45 sets, each with three long trailers, for services from Gare de Lyon to Melun and Malsherbes. Its earlier members of the class, with short trailers, were sent to Vitry and Les Joncherelles. These were then used to replace hauled stock on the shuttle from Saint-Lazare to Nanterre and on the Nord's service to Persan-Beaumont. Sets are numbered in sequence from 20501/20502 to 20737/20738.

In 1994 it was the turn of Les Joncherolles to receive new sets, in four coach formation, for use on line D. Extra trailers were delivered at this time, to allow for future expansion of services on that line; in the meantime, they were used behind locomotives on services to Château-Thierry.

The deliveries of 1996/97 saw the class appearing for the first time on services from Gare de l'Est, when ten four-coach and two five-coach sets were stabled at the new facilities at Noisy-le-Sec.

Vitry also received some additional sets to replace some of class Z5300 when these were sent off to provincial service. Finally Les Joncherolles received six additional five coach sets for use on line D in place of some of the first delivery, which were then cascaded to services to Persan-Beaumont and Pontoise, replacing the last of the 1960 hauled stock.

In 1998 an additional 32 four coach units were ordered for delivery in 2000/01. These will be used to replace class Z5300 on line C. The new trains will differ from earlier batches in having Onix traction equipment, regenerative braking and air conditioning of both the driving cab and passenger accommodation. In the interest of security, it will also be possible to close off the motor coaches to passengers in late evening trains.

All motor coaches were built by Alsthom and all trailers by ANF Industries.

Dates of delivery:

1988	Z20501/02
1989/90	Z20503/04 – Z20583/84
1991	Z20585/86 – Z20625/26
1992/93	Z20627/28 – Z20713/14
1994	Z20715/16 – Z20763/64
1996/97	Z20765/66 – Z20887/88

Names are carried as follows:

20501/20502 LE PLESSIS-BOUCHARD	20513/20514 VILLIERS-LE-BEL
20531/20532 BEAUCHAMP	20871/20872 SAVIGNY-SUR-ORGE
20863/20864 EPINAY-SUR-ORGE	

An experimental stainless steel trailer is incorporated in set 20589/90 of Vitry.

All three classes of double-deck motor coach can work in multiple with each other, although this is not normally done in passenger service. Following experiments, it is likely that all units will be fitted with air conditioning in the driving cab as they fall due for overhaul over the next few years.

To assist staff with identification, sets also carry a code, which is given in white on the red band just below the windscreen. This code is made up of the set number followed by a letter; these letters carry the following identification:

C	Courant continu	(direct current)	class 5600
B	Bi-courant	(dual voltage)	class 8800
A	Asynchrone	(asynchronous)	class 20500 not used on line D
V	Villeneuve	Class 20500 stabled at that depot for line D	
J	Les Joncherolles	"	"	"	"

Trailers built to work with class Z20500 came in two types, all-second class and composite. The former are numbered ZRBe 201501–201887 and 203501–203885, while the latter are numbered 202501–202887.

As of January 1999, the total fleet of double-deck multiple units of type Z2N (excluding sets in course of delivery) was 304, being made up of 608 motor coaches and 743 trailers. This represents approximately half of all suburban material in Ile-de-France. All three classes have proved to be successful in service and excellent crowd movers, not only in regular operation but also on special occasions such as the World Cup in 1998 or the visit of the Pope to Rheims in 1996, when some sets of class Z20500 were loaned from Paris to cope with the crowds. In the summer of 1999 three four coach sets of this class were sent to Avignon to help with holiday traffic in Provence, but on longer services these met with a mixed reception.

MS61 STOCK

This class was constructed for line A only, although some sets operated on line B when first delivered.

Class MS61 is made up of three-coach sets, two motors enclosing a trailer, and in service can be made up into trains of one, two or three units. There were in all 127 sets delivered in six batches between 1967 and 1980 and divided into sub-classes A to E and EX. Construction was divided between the firms of Brissoneau et Lotz, ANF and CIMT, but the bogies for all sets were made by ANF. The motor coaches of the first 62 sets (sub-classes A and B) have three-section panoramic windscreens but, as with the Glasgow 'Blue Trains', it was found that this attractive feature was difficult to maintain and the later 65 sets have a smaller one-piece panoramic windscreen. A panel for display of the headcode is fitted above the windscreen.

Internally the trains are very much of their period, with extensive use of plastic panelling, in light beige, and fluorescent lighting. Forced ventilation is fitted. Originally motor coaches were second class only, the accommodation in the trailers being divided equally between the classes; the former can accommodate 62 seated passengers plus 32 on strapontins, the latter 72 plus 32. Standing capacity, at four persons per square metre, is officially 111 per coach, but in practice this is often exceeded by up to 66% and a total capacity of 858 passengers per set has become the norm. Four double-width doors per side, each with a clear opening of 1.30m, allowed what was expected to be more than sufficient room for the exchange of passengers, although in practice this was later found to be inadequate. Class MS61 was the first to display the RER blue and light grey livery, which was replaced by the present red/white/blue in the late 1980s.

A train of MS61 A/B stock leaves Vincennes heading west at Saint-Mandé on 22 July 2000.
Brian Patton

Motor coaches are fitted with four Oerlikon nose-suspended 200kW motors, permanently coupled in series on each bogie. JH controllers are provided. Both air and rheostatic brakes are fitted, the latter being independent of the traction motors. Motor coaches are 23.8m long and trailers 23.5m and unladen weights are 57 and 34 tonnes respectively. Scharfenberg automatic couplings are fitted, those within each set being modified to accommodate the traction current and air supply. RATP engineers drew on their experience with these couplings in the articulated stock of the Metro to ensure that there would be fewer problems with the MS61 stock. There are two systems of suspension – rubber blocks provide the primary suspension and steel resorts the secondary and there are also shock absorbers. Monobloc wheels and roller bearing axle boxes also help to give a ride of a very good standard. Although designed for driver-only operation, with a form of 'dead man's handle' on the controller, many sets ran initially with a guard and it was not until 1976 that all ran as originally intended. Later the class was also fitted with equipment for the SACEM system (*q.v.*).

A set of the later design of MS61 displays its single-piece windscreen at Boissy Saint-Léger in May 1992. *Brian Hardy*

A contrast in front ends of class MS61B (left) and MS61E (right) at Rueil-Malmaison in May 1994. *Brian Hardy*

A view of the interior of a composite trailer of class MS61 after refurbishment. *Brian Hardy*

The first sets went into service on line B on 29 June 1967 and ultimately 25 sets were in operation there. Not only did this give a chance to test the new trains in service but it also brought some relief to the overworked and overcrowded Z stock. Later sets entered service on line A as successive parts of it were opened and by 1981, with the arrival of class MI79, class MS61 was concentrated on its home ground and it has remained there since. Normally the class operates mainly on the Boissy-Saint-Léger – Saint-Germain service, with peak hour extras between La Défense and Torcy. Technically, it has been a successful design but operationally it has been unable to cope with the tremendous growth of traffic, leading to frequent and prolonged overcrowding. This in turn led to excessive speed in the rotation of the motors, causing them to wear out prematurely. By 1988 all trains needed some attention and half the sets had to be given an extra-heavy overhaul. But it would have been unrealistic to have expected the designers in the early 1960s to have foreseen the success of line A and class MS61 should not be judged a failure because of its later problems.

A train to Boissy-Saint-Léger, formed of MS61 C, D or E stock runs in to Sucy-Bonneuil on 22 July 2000. *Brian Patton*

Construction and delivery of class MS61 sets:

MS61A   1967

M15001–15018, M15043/44, M15055–15065
AB18001–18005, AB18014/19, AB18033–18039, AB18043–18045

MS61B   1969

M15019–15042, M15045–15054, M15066–15124
AB18006–18013, AB18015–18018, AB18020–18034, AB18043–18045

MS61C   1970/71

M15125–15148, AB18061–18072

MS61D   1973/74

M15149–15216, AB18073–18106

MS61E   1977

M15217–15236, AB18107–18119

MS61EX   1980

M15237–15254, AB18120–18128

Paris has not escaped the tide of graffiti which has become a menace in many cities over the past two decades, public transport often suffering badly and many measures were taken to maintain rolling stock in a tidy and presentable state. One experiment was the application of the Ile-de-France livery on a "random" basis, as seen on MS61 trailer AB18048 at Sucy-Bonneuil on line A. While successful in deterring the graffiti hooligans, this particular design was not adopted for the fleet. *Brian Hardy*

An interior view of a coach of class MI84. Diagonally opposite pairs of seats have been removed to create more circulating space. *Brian Hardy*

CLASS MI84

This is an improved version of class MI79 (see next chapter), ordered and owned by RATP alone, although two sets were loaned to SNCF between July 1987 and May 1988 and a further two for a brief period in 1992. It was delivered from March 1986 to September 1988 and a further 18 units, classed MI84B, were placed in service between April 1989 and January 1990.

The main difference from the earlier class lies in the electronic control system. On the first delivery, now known as class MI84A, the chopper control equipment is smaller and lighter than in class MI79, weighing only 1255kg compared with 1550kg. A fluid cooling system has also removed the need for forced ventilation of both this equipment and the static convector. The process was further developed in class MI84B, the need for coolant being reduced and allowing the weight to come down to 800kg. Maximum speed has, however, been reduced to 120km/hr.

Internally, the new class may be distinguished by the red and blue check seating, and by the continuous lighting strip which has replaced the separate fixtures. To provide more room in the vestibules, the small 'appui troncs' (leaning posts) have been replaced by a single vertical grab rail. Ceilings are at a constant height, rather than being split, and the luggage racks have gone. These refinements give a much less cluttered internal appearance as well as improving passenger circulation and decreasing noise. Rather strangely, in view of contemporary concerns about security, the interconnexion between coaches of class MI79 was not repeated on its successor.

The entire class was built by GEC-Alsthom, who also supplied the electrical equipment. The bogies were made by ANF Industrie.

MI84 stock is numbered in sequence as follows:

8341	28341	28342	8342	8341/2 are named BOISSY SAINT LÉGER
to				8413/4 are named POISSY
8485	29485	28486	8486	8441/2 are named INTERLAKEN

RER STOCK USED BY BOTH RATP AND SNCF

CLASS MI79 – SNCF CLASS Z8100

This class was the first designed to run on the lines of both operators. It is therefore dual-voltage – 1,500 dc and 25kV ac – and it can also be used to serve platforms of different heights, namely 1m and 1.10m on RATP sections and .50m, .80m and 1m on SNCF sections.

By the time this class was designed, even off-peak traffic had grown to the extent that three-coach sets were inadequate and it was decided to provide at least four coaches at all times of the day. The formation is two motor coaches at the outer ends of a set and two intermediate trailers, one of which is a composite. The maximum formation in normal RER service is two sets. Scharfenberg couplings are fitted at the outer ends of a set and and bar couplings between vehicles within a set. Sets can be split and worked in halves but this is done only for works purposes and not in normal passenger service.

The bodywork is constructed of extruded aluminium and the coach sides are slightly curved to give maximum width, which at floor level is 2.8m. Overall length is 26m for both motor and trailers coaches and unladen weights are 56 and 48 tonnes respectively. For the first time in RER stock, gangway communication allows passengers to circulate within a set. As with class MS 61 there are four double-width doors per side, each with a clear opening of 1.30m. To serve stations with lower platforms, the step plate can be moved by the driver to a lower position. Should this fail to operate properly, opening of the doors is impossible. Within each coach, glass screens separate groups of seats and there are no internal doors, not even between first and second class areas.

Coach 8137 is at the rear of a northbound train at Denfert Rochereau when almost new in June 1980. *Brian Patton*

An interior view of a coach of class MI79. *Brian Hardy*

As it was thought important to provide as many seats as possible, there are three bays of seats between each set of doors and vestibules are in consequence rather cramped. Despite this, strapontins are fitted on the right of each door, but if these are in use at busy stations, their occupants do run the risk of having their toes trodden on! Total seating capacity of a set is 312 plus 160 on strapontins. Standing capacity, at four passengers per square metre, is 531, though this figure can be attained only if the strapontins are not used.

To distinguish the new stock, it was decided to adopt a new livery, the blue and grey being now considered rather bland, and class MI79 was the first to appear in the now-familiar blue, red and white livery. This requires careful cleaning if it is to retain its sparkle and it has to be said that the teams of both operators have risen to the challenge – dirty trains are not seen in service. There was also a desire to provide a livelier internal colour scheme and bright yellow was adopted for the panelling, seats being in alternate groups of red and royal blue.

Inter-communication between driver and passengers is provided, this being another 'first' for the class.

The electrical equipment, including the pantograph, is located in one of the trailers. Each motor coach is fitted with four 350kW motors, two being attached to the central beam of each bogie. Maximum speed is 140km/hr. Thyristor control is provided and there are both air and electric brakes, the latter being capable of regenerating on 1500V dc lines. The rheostatic brake can be used only on 25kV ac lines. Electronic control allows deceleration independent of the laden weight of the train. The normal VACMA dead man's control is fitted, as well as a train protection system which will activate the emergency brake in the event of non-observance by the driver. Changeover from one voltage to another is carried out automatically.

Delivery of this stock was by a series of joint orders, of which the first, for 110 sets for RATP and 42 for SNCF, was placed on 29 June 1976. The first set was delivered to the workshop at Massy-Palaiseau on 5 October 1979 and the class was placed in traffic on 28 May 1980 on line B. Delivery was completed by 1983. Later orders for what became class MI79B brought the total number of sets to 193 by 1984, of which 51 are owned by SNCF. Trains do carry the name of their owner beside the RER logo, but it is in small print and one has to look closely to distinguish one from another.

Theoretically SNCF units are allocated to La Chapelle depot, but regardless of ownership all units are maintained at Massy. All sets were built by the Sociéte Franco-Belge de Matériel de Chemin de Fer with electrical equipment by CEM-Oerlikon and bogies by ANF.

Unfortunately there were initial and rather prolonged teething troubles when this class entered service. The converters on the trailers were noisy and had to be modified, there were air bursts and the piping had to be replaced by a system of locked pipes and the electronic equipment had to be altered to lessen interference with other systems. In January 1987 other problems occurred when 10 cm of snow fell in a very short time and much of this found its way into the equipment, causing trains to freeze up where they stood. As a result service on line B was suspended from 14 to 19 January. At a cost of FR11.2 million, the control equipment was then sealed and the ventilation to the choppers was altered to cut out when temperatures fell to –2 degrees.

Since then the class has proved to be extremely successful.

Two trains of class MI79 display the logos of their respective owners at Saint-Rémy.
Brian Hardy

The nameplate and badge of class MI79 ZBD8261 (SNCF owned) MITRY-MORY.
Brian Hardy

Numbering and ownership of units of class MI79:

RATP units				SNCF units			
8101	28101	28102	8102	8103	28103	28104	8104
8105	28105	28106	8106	8121	28121	28122	8122
in sequence to				8125	28125	28126	8126
8119	28119	28120	8120	8127	28127	28128	8128
8123	28123	28124	8124	8131	28131	28132	8132
8129	28129	28130	8130	8133	28133	28134	8134
8137	28137	28138	8138	8135	28135	28136	8136
8145	28145	28146	8146	8139	28139	28140	8140
8153	28153	28154	8154	*in sequence to*			
8161	28161	28162	8162	8143	28143	28144	8144
8169	28169	28170	8170	8147	28147	28148	8148
8177	28177	28178	8178	*in sequence to*			
8187	28187	28188	8188	8151	28152	28152	8152
8193	28193	28194	8194	*in sequence to*			
8195	28195	28196	8196	8155	28155	28156	8156
8201	28201	28202	8202	*in sequence to*			
8203	28203	28204	8204	8159	28159	28160	8160
8209	28209	28210	8210	8163	28163	28164	8164
8211	28211	28212	8212	*in sequence to*			
8217	28217	28218	8218	8167	28167	28168	8168
8219	28219	28220	8220	8171	28171	28172	8172
8225	28225	28226	8226	*in sequence to*			
8227	28227	28228	8228	8175	28175	28176	8176
8229	28229	28230	8230	8179	28179	28180	8180
8233	28233	28234	8234	*in sequence to*			
8235	28235	28236	8236	8185	28185	28186	8186
8241	28241	28242	8242	8189	28189	28190	8190
8265	28265	28266	8266	8191	28191	28192	8192
in sequence to				8197	28197	28198	8198
8339	28339	28340	8340	8199	28199	28200	8200
				8205	28205	28206	8206
Some sets are named as follows:				8207	28207	28208	8208
8121/2 ÉPINAY-SUR-SEINE				8213	28213	28214	8214
8257/8 RAISMES				8215	28215	28216	8216
8261/2 MITRY-MORY				8221	28221	28222	8222
8263/4 PERSAN				8223	28223	28224	8224
				8231	28231	28232	8232
				8237	28237	28238	8238
				8239	28239	28240	8240
				8243	28243	28244	8244
				in sequence to			
				8263	28263	28264	8264

CLASS MI2N – Z22500

While all the above classes have been successful, it was thought that for service on line E some changes were required in the basic design of rolling stock. As capacity had increased, station dwell times had lengthened in proportion. It has also been recognised that RER services are now catering for two discrete groups of passenger, with quite different needs. The passenger travelling a relatively long distance from a suburb to the central area requires a reasonably quiet and spacious atmosphere in which to read or work, while those making short journeys, especially within Paris, are more concerned with entry and exit facilities and having adequate standing room. In all previous stock there is no obvious spatial separation of these two groups and passengers settling down for a longer journey are jostled by those travelling for one or two stations. Nor are any of these classes easy of access for persons of reduced mobility, whether their difficulty arises from a physical impairment or an impediment such as heavy luggage. In short, while technically successful, existing stock, as recorded in various surveys of passenger opinion, is not seen as especially user-friendly.

For service on line E, SNCF required a high capacity multiple unit, which would have enhanced performance compared with earlier stock and which would also provide greater comfort for the travelling public. Given existing platform lengths and the impossibility of extending these, a double-deck design was the only possible solution. At the same time, RATP was seeking to expand still further the capacity of line A and it seemed that a double-deck design could be a solution to the problems experienced there. It was therefore decided to adopt a joint design, with a few modifications to suit the special characteristics of line A service.

The experimental two door trailer, MI2N 18202, at Boissy depot on 6 May 1992. *Brian Hardy*

With these considerations in mind, both operators engaged the firm of MBD Design to carry out market research on vehicle design and this ultimately took the form of two new double-deck trailer coaches which were placed in service on line A early in 1991. These were built by GEC-Alsthom. One had two and one three double doors per side. It was found that in service the station dwell times were the same as for a single-deck coach with four doors per side. A survey of passenger opinion brought favourable comments and passengers especially mentioned ease of boarding and alighting compared with existing stock. They also mentioned the pleasure of viewing the passing scene from the upper deck. Between the two prototypes, it appeared that more passengers preferred that with three doors, with regard to both ease of entry and exit and movement within the coach. The way was clear for use of this design on line A. The two prototypes have since been scrapped.

Both operators then created a working party to develop the new concept and at the end of 1992 a joint order was placed with GEC-Alsthom for 70 units, of which 53 were for SNCF. Two pre-production sets entered service in the autumn of 1996 and delivery was completed in 1998. The description given here is for SNCF stock, the modifications in RATP stock being detailed later.

An interior view of the three-door version. *Brian Hardy*

A close up view of a train of class MI2N stock on line A, showing the peach colour scheme adopted for the interiors. "Plug" type doors, which open outwards and slide backwards against the car body, are a feature of these units. *Brian Hardy*

The main aim of the designers was to maximise capacity and in this they have been extremely successful. A five coach rake of this design can carry 1280 passengers, of whom 550 are seated and 730 standing. This represents an increase of 46% in total capacity over earlier stock. For the first time, three sets of double doors, each with a clear opening of 2m, have been provided in each side of every coach and it is estimated that this arrangement allows 550 passengers to enter or leave within 50 seconds. Retractable steps are fitted to cope with lower platform heights in some stations, although it is still cannot be claimed that the trains are fully accessible to everyone.

The provision of three doors allows, to a certain extent, a natural separation of different groups of passengers. Instead of the through lower and upper saloons seen in earlier classes, class MI2N has two discrete saloons on each level, but while the lower saloons are accessible from each of the three vestibules, the upper saloons can be reached from the end vestiblues only, and so have stairs at the outer ends only. It is intended that these areas will offer a more restful environment for those travelling some distance, while the lower saloons will cater for short-distance passengers.

The trains are again dual-voltage and can operate on 1500V dc or 25kV ac. Maximum speed is 140km/hr, though normal service speed on urban sections is 60–80km/hr. With almost 3000kW available per set, acceleration is rapid and the class is capable of tackling gradients of 28% at 60km/hr when fully loaded. Regenerative braking is fitted. From the environmental point of view, it should be noted that a train made up of two fully-loaded sets will consume only the equivalent of .25 litre of petrol per 100km, while a private car for the same distance, and assuming a passenger load of 1.5 persons, will consume 7 litres. Class MI2N is environmentally friendly!

The driving cab is air-conditioned and closed-circuit television has been installed. Passenger areas have pressure ventilation. Ergonomically designed seating of an entirely new type is fitted, upholstered in brown vandal-resistant fabric and panelling is salmon pink, in both saloons and vestibules. One of the trailers has space for passengers with disabilities, though in view of the problem of platform heights mentioned above, access is not equally easy at every station. There is through access between the three vehicles in the middle of a set to allow passengers to reach the toilet which is located in the central second class trailer.

The driving trailers are 22.85m long, while intermediate coaches are 22.1m long. Normal formation of a five-coach set is driving trailer, motor coach with space for passengers with disabilities, trailer with toilet, motor coach and driving trailer. Each driving trailer is fitted with a pantograph.

The class is painted in a modified version of the Ile-de-France livery, although two sets received a special livery for use on inaugural trains on the opening day of line E.

To test public reaction and also to iron out teething troubles some sets were used on peak hour working from Saint-Lazare to Maisons-Lafitte between November 1998 and June 1999.

SNCF stock is numbered consecutively as follows:

221501   22501   222501   22502   221502
in sequence to
221601   22602   222601   22602   221602

Sets are not normally separated, even for maintenance.

The most obvious internal difference in RATP stock is that access to both levels is available from each vestibule, to speed up loading and unloading and if possible to maintain a station dwell time of only 50 seconds. For the same reason, the proportion of seated to standing passengers is slightly different (528/763). The backs of the seats are distinctly more upright. Despite the length of some journeys which can be made on line A, no toilet is fitted. As all platforms on the line are of the same (high) level, there is no need for the retractable steps fitted to SNCF sets.

To maintain the schedules envisaged for line A in future, an additional motor coach is fitted in RATP sets, whose formation is two driving trailers and three intermediate motors. Total power available is 3700kW per set and maximum acceleration is 1.1m/second. Equipment for SACEM has also been fitted. It is technically possible for RATP sets to work on SNCF lines with high platforms and vice versa, though as SNCF stock is not fitted for SACEM, it is unlikely that it will ever be seen on line A. The first sets entered revenue service on line A on 6 June 1997. Passenger reaction has been positive, although there have been problems with the door mechanism which required trains to be withdrawn from service for modification. Passengers when travelling within the central area have shown a tendency to stand in the vestibules, thus impeding the entry and exit of others and the expected dwell times in central area stations have not yet been reached. However, sets have in general preformed well and have brought a new standard of comfort for commuters on line E and a lessening of overcrowding for those on line A.

In July 1999 an additional twelve sets were ordered from Alstom and Bombardier for delivery from February 2001.

RATP stock is numbered as follows:

1501   2501   3501   2502   1502
in sequence to
1533   2533   3533   2534   1534

OTHER SNCF SUBURBAN STOCK

LOCOMOTIVE HAULED STOCK

RIB STOCK

These initials stand for Rame Inoxydable de Banlieue or Stainless Steel Suburban Set. These sets work all over Ile-de-France except on the south east lines and were the predecessors of class Z5300 multiple units.

These coaches are also based on classes Z23700 and Z5100 and were also built by Carel et Fouché. The first went into service in 1961 operating as eight-coach trains from Gare du Nord to Creil and from 1963 they were also used on services from Gare de l'Est to Gargan and Meaux. The sets on the latter could be divided into two four coach sets for off-peak working. Although the public appreciated the comfort of upholstered seats in second class, there were complaints about rough riding, this being due to the small diameter of the wheels. The problem was tackled by fitting pneumatic suspension to 239 further vehicles delivered in 1970. These went to the Est, for electrification to Tournan, to the Nord, Montparnasse, and Saint-Lazare. Further sets were delivered between 1976 and 1980. Finally, between 1981 and 1984, 171 additional coaches were placed in service on outer-suburban work. These are actually classified RIO (Rame Inox Omnibus) and have individually configured seats; in practice, all coaches are used interchangeably. The total numbers of each type were 400 RIB and 250 RIO. In recent years some have been withdrawn and others sent off to provincial services, leaving, in 1997, 539 in Ile-de-France.

Units are formed of three or four coaches, with a maximum of nine coaches per train. A four coach set provides 480 seats and a maximum capacity of 666 passengers, this figure being calculated on three standing passengers per square metre. Each coach is fitted with a toilet. Maximum speed is 120km/hr. They are not equipped for one-person operation and in normal service the guard travels in the leading coach.

While these sets now in use give a smooth ride and are reasonably accessible from low platforms, they do not have either the capacity or comfort for present-day service and are likely to be replaced within the next few years.

Some RIB locomotive-hauled stock is still used on services from Gare de l'Est. With unit 402 at the rear, a rake of this stock stands at Les Bouillereaux – Champigny in July 1999. *Brian Patton*

CLASS VB2N

These initials denote Voiture Banlieue à Deux Niveaux or Double Deck Suburban Stock

In the face of ever-growing suburban traffic, even on non-electrified lines, the État decided in 1930 to re-introduce the double-deck concept of rolling stock, in modern all-metal form. In 1932 an order was placed with the Entreprises Industrielles Charentaises for ten eight-coach units, each offering a total capacity of 2040 passengers. This compared with 1524 passengers in a nine-coach set of standard bogie stock. A further series of forty units was delivered in 1934, construction this time being divided between the Entreprises Charentaises and Carel et Fouché. Despite a few problems with the steps at the doorways they proved successful in service, and in 1937 some were adapted for use with electric locomotives out of Montparnasse. The last was not withdrawn until 1983 and one has been preserved. These sets were the predecessors of all modern European double-deck stock.

A rake of VB2N stock heads a Gare de l'Est – Meaux train past Chelles-Gournay in June 1997.
David Haydock

In the early 1970s, it became clear that certain suburban lines were reaching saturation point and that it would become necessary to find paths for additional trains if demand were to be met. These paths could only be found through greatly increased expenditure on new tracks and associated works, and SNCF managers, in co-operation with industry, began to consider the alternative of introducing a new generation of double-deck suburban stock. The result of these discussions was class VB2N, of which the first examples went into service on 2 June 1975 between Saint-Lazare and Pointoise.

A total of 530 coaches of this design was subsequently built between 1975 and 1979, and a further batch of 59 followed between 1980 and 1984. Apart from two which have been withdrawn following accident damage, all are still in service and can be seen on all lines except those in the south east. Trains are normally worked in sets of eight coaches, though four coach sets may be run in off-peak periods. An eight coach set carries 1320 seated and 572 standing passengers.

Between 1993 and 1997, all of class VB2N were adapted for one-person operation. Entry and exit are by double doors, each with a clear opening of 1.8m, located over the bogies. From the vestibules, straight stairs lead up and down to the saloons. Seating is 3+2, originally on bench-type seats, though in some sets these have now been replaced by individual seats. Additional seats are fitted in the vestibules, except in the driving trailers, in which case a cab occupies one end. Each coach has a toilet.

Livery was originally grey with a broad orange band below the lower deck windows and a similar one, edged by two narrow black bands between the two decks. This scheme was striking when new and was certainly a great improvement on both the dreary green of older stock or the colourless appearance of stainless steel stock, but it tended to fade and is many coaches now carry the regional livery.

There are also 100 coaches built with individual seats between 1980 and 1981 and classified VO2N (double-deck omnibus stock) for outer-suburban services. In practice, all coaches are now used on any service.

This design, which picked up where the État had left off in the 1930s, represented a quantum leap forward in the design of suburban stock and from it has been derived all subsequent designs of multiple unit trains used in Ile-de-France, as well as in some provincial areas. It has also been exported to Italy where identical trains are in use on both FS and FNM (Ferrovie Nord Milano) lines, and has directly inspired similar stock on other systems such as NS and SNCB. Class VB2N must be considered to have been one of the classic coach designs of the twentieth century.

MULTIPLE UNITS

There are three classes which do not operate on RER lines, collectively known as 'Inoxydables' of 'Inox' (stainless steel) sets. These are derived from class Z5100 of 1954, none of which now remains in service. In all cases, the last three digits of the set number are displayed in the offside front window.

CLASS Z6100

These are three coach units used on services from Gare du Nord, sometimes running beyond Ile-de-France to destinations such as Amiens. Three prototypes were built in 1960/61 as class Z6000 but series production did not begin until 1965 and continued until 1971. These sets run on 25kV ac lines only. A set consists of a driving motor, and two trailers. The motor coach has a single monomotor bogie with a 690kW motor, giving a maximum speed of 120km/hr. Total seating capacity is 280. A few sets have now been withdrawn and some have been sold to Luxembourg, leaving 228 in service in the Paris area in January 1999.

Production series numbers were from:

6101 26101   16101
in sequence to
6184 26184   16184

CLASS Z6300

This series is a development of the above for use on services from Saint-Lazare and was built from 1967 to 1970. To cope with the tighter curves found on the western lines, they are slightly shorter and are not gangwayed throughout. They are also less powerful, as the motor is of 615kW only.

Adjustable steps are fitted to cope with different platform heights. In all other respects this class is identical to class Z6100. Some sets have now been transferred away from Paris leaving in 1998 only twelve operating out of Saint-Lazare.

Numbers were originally as follows:

6301 26301   16301
in sequence to
6335 26335   16335

CLASS Z6400

These were the last stainless steel units built and were introduced for the re-electrification of the Saint-Lazare suburban network between 1976 and 1979. They may be distinguished from earlier classes by the broad blue band around the windows and a more raked windscreen. They are formed into four-coach sets, of which they first and last vehicles are motor coaches. The use of mono-motor bogies was discontinued with this class and each motor coach has four 295kW motors.

Some sets are arranged to work only on those lines which have high platforms at stations (Versailles RD and Marly) while others work on the line to Poissy which has low platforms only. The class is currently receiving mid-life overhaul and is being repainted into the latest livery.

Numbers are:

```
6401  26401   26402   6402
 in sequence to
6540  26549   26550   6550
```

Sets 6441/42 to 6523/24 inclusive are used on high platform lines.

Certain sets are named, as follows:

6447/48 CHAVILLE	6449/50 COURBVOIE
6457/58 LOUVECIENNES	6485/86 GARCHES
6505/06 VAUCRESSON	6519/20 LA CELLE-SAINT CLOUD
6523/24 MARLY-LE-ROI	6549/50 LA GARENNE-COLOMBES
6471/72 SAINT-NOM-LA- BRETÈCHE	6475/76 L'ÉTANG-LA-VILLE

The Z6400 EMUs working out of Saint-Lazare are now being refurbished, one such example being seen on 15 October 2000 at Nanterre Université. The livery adopted is a modified version of the Ile de France colours seen on other RER lines. The red door colour, for example, stops at waist level, so that the white beneath provides a nearer match with the stainless steel bodysides below waist level. Not the 'Transilien' logo on the front. *Brian Hardy*

An interior of a refurbished Z6400 EMU. Whilst the refurbishment is very much a cosmetic job – i.e. both refurbished and non-refurbished sets are able to work together – the transformation is striking. Most of the interior seating is 2+2 as seen here, and the drab brown and cream colour scheme has been replaced. *Brian Hardy*

LOCOMOTIVES

Various classes of electric locomotive are employed on Paris suburban services.

CLASS 816500

These are BB locomotives built between 1958 and 1964 and now based at La Villette for use on Est suburban services. They have monomotor bogies and two Alsthom motors giving an output of 2580kW.

CLASS 817000

These are also BB locomotives. The class, which totals 105, was built by Alsthom between 1965 and 1968 and is almost entirely confined to Paris suburban work from Nord, Est and Saint-Lazare. All are fitted for push-pull operation. Two Alsthom motors give an output of 2940kW. Some have been equipped for one-person operation on Est services.

CLASS 825500

This is a dual-voltage version of class 817000. The class was built between 1964 and 1976 by Alsthom and was initially designed for freight service. However, a number have since been fitted with push-pull equipment for suburban services.

CLASS 9600

On 1500V dc lines from Montparnasse, some trains are worked by class 8500, which is a dc version of class 17000 and was also built by Alsthom between 1966 and 1974.

Other classes may occasionally be seen on outer-suburban trains.

WORKS LOCOMOTIVES

Seven locomotives built to work the freight trains had much in common with Z stock, having the same type of motors and control equipment, and with double-width centre doors they also looked like shortened passenger coaches. However, there were four JH motors, mounted two on each bogie, giving an output of 744kW, and the control system was modified to allow prolonged running at slow speed. Maximum speed was again 80km/hr. They were constructed by the Compagnie Générale des Constructions in 1937 and were double-ended. Length was 11.48m and weight was 54 tonnes. Although fully capable of coping with a freight train single-handed, they were always worked in pairs during the hours of passenger service, to avoid delays in the event of a failure.

The locomotives were painted in the same livery as the passenger stock for many years. At various dates between 1973 and 1988 they were repainted yellow. Despite the demise of freight operation, all remained on the active roster and several are still employed on works trains on both lines A and B.

There was also a steam locomotive acquired by the CMP in 1942 – presumably its only such – for use in some non-electrified sidings and on work trains when the power was off at night. It was an 0–4–0 saddle tank (0–2–0T in French numbering), built in the USA by Baldwin in 1914. It had its hour of glory in June 1944 when it was able to rescue some stranded motor coaches from the danger area at Massy. Its end was rather pathetic; during an overhaul in 1950, the coupling rods were removed and put to one side, near a pile of old iron. A tidy individual then sent the lot to the scrap heap and, bereft of its rods, the little locomotive could only follow down the same road. It was replaced by a more powerful diesel-electric locomotive, T101, which was similar to class C61000 of SNCF, having three coupled axles, a Sulzer diesel of 785kW and to electric motors. Between 1973 and 1975, seven further machines of the same class were bought from SNCF and became T104–T109 and T130.

DEPOTS AND WORKSHOPS

Only the lines of the RER operated by RATP have dedicated depots and workshops. On SNCF lines these facilities are shared with other stock, both suburban and main line.

Prior to the electrification of the Sceaux line, locomotives were shedded at the depot of Paris-Denfert and it was on the site of this that a new depot was built for the electric stock. Built between 1936 and 1939 and known as Montrouge, this complex was originally intended to cope with 75 coaches of Z stock and had to be enlarged considerably in 1965 to cater for the increased fleet. However, due to the built-up nature of the surrounding area, there was no room for further expansion and it was decided to build an additional depot and workshops complex at Massy-Palaiseau. This is located to the north of the station, between RATP and SNCF lines and consists of a maintenance area and a cleaning area. It was opened in 1969. Montrouge carried out the last overhauls on Z stock c1985 then for a few years undertook upgrading of class MS61. It has now been closed and the site redeveloped.

MI2N unit Z1524/1523 in the company of MI84 stock at Torcy depot. *David Haydock*

In Boissy depot in January 1989 motor coach ZBD8116 is under maintenance. Note the double doors in the end of the coach, which allow passengers to move to an adjacent coach in MI79 stock. *Brian Hardy*

The main depot of the Vincennes line was located at Nogent-sur-Marne but it was decided that, for the opening of the RER, it would be preferable to close this and build a completely new depot and workshop to cater for the MS61 fleet. This is located at Boissy-Saint-Léger and covers an area of 40,000 square metres, with a yard of twenty sidings for storage. The facilities comprise workshops catering for both routine maintenance and heavy overhauls as well as a cleaning area. There is also accommodation for track maintenance equipment and electrical services. New stock on trial is also based at Boissy and its facilities have also been used for refurbishment of Métro stock of both classes MF67 and MP73.

The other depots for line A are situated at Rueil, on the site of a former SNCF depot for Standard stock, and at Torcy. The former houses approximately half the stock of line A and is responsible for routine maintenance; it was opened in 1969. The completion of this facility while third rail trains were still running was difficult and problems with its construction were largely responsible for the delays in the opening of service on this part of Line A. The new depot and workshop at Torcy were opened in April 1992.

SNCF stock operating on line B is based at Paris La Chapelle and maintained at Massy. The oldest depot in Paris, La Chapelle was originally built for the Nord company in 1846 and it may be closed in the fairly near future. The buildings at present used for suburban stock were constructed in the 1950s to house diesel railcars and were extended in the 1960s to accommodate the first units of class Z6100. With the arrival of class Z20500, its facilities were deemed no longer adequate and a new depot was opened at Les Joncherolles, north of Saint-Denis.

Coach M15192 of class MS61D stands on the traverser outside Boissy depot after refurbishment in January 1989. *Brian Hardy*

A view of Boissy depot on 9 January 1989, with a Sceaux line electric locomotive and trains of classes MI79 and MS61. *Brian Hardy*

On line C, class Z5300 is stabled at Vitry-Les Ardoines, located south-east of Paris Austerlitz. This depot was opened in 1969 to replace the former facilities at Paris-Masséna and has been twice enlarged, in 1974 and 1987. It also houses all 58 dual-voltage sets of class Z8800 and 36 sets of class Z5600 (those with two trailers). There are also 52 sets of class Z20500 stock, including the 21 sets which incorporate two short trailers.

The other 6 units of class Z5600, with four trailers, are shedded at Villeneuve-Saint-Georges for use on services from Gare de Lyon. Villeneuve, located about ten kilometres south-east of Gare de Lyon, dates back to PLM days and received its first electric trains in 1951, when a specialised workshop was constructed for class Z5100. It was enlarged in 1973 to provide maintenance facilities for class Z5300 sets. Further extensions, to accommodate double-deck stock, were made in 1983 and 1995. It is also home to 48 sets of class Z20500 used on line D. Like Vitry, it also deals with main line stock.

Classes Z6300 and Z6400 operating from Saint-Lazare are shedded at Saint-Lazare-Levallois. This depot was erected in the 1960s on the site of a former workshop.

Although no special depot facilities were provided by SNCF when lines C and D opened, this has not been the case with line E. The suburban lines radiating from Gare de l'Est had, until the arrival of class Z20500 in 1995, been worked entirely by locomotive hauled stock, both double- and single-deck. The locomotives were shedded at La Villette, while the rolling stock was housed at Paris Ourcq, both depots dating from 1930 and by the 1970s no longer adequate, especially as both had to accommodate main line stock also. A new maintenance facility was therefore opened in 1975 at Noisy-le-Sec, where the workshops, dating from 1913, had just been vacated. However, even this facility was considered unsuitable for dealing with the new trains for line E.

The number of sidings was therefore increased from 15 to 19 and a slight adaptation to the head of these allowed the storage of five coach sets of class Z20500. On close examination, it was evident that it would cost more to adapt the existing workshop building than to replace it completely by a new facility, which would better serve future needs. It was therefore demolished in 1994 and in its place a new building was erected, having ten roads and fitted with the most modern equipment. The number of roads can later be increased to 13 or even 16 to cater for the TGV stock of the Est line when that comes into service about 2006. From the technical angle, the main novelty of the workshop is the facility which allows a complete set of classes Z20500 and MI2N to be lifted as a whole for maintenance. As there is considerable electrical interconnexion between vehicles, the previous practice of lifting individual coaches is no longer suitable. These new facilities were brought into use in 1997 and occupy an area of 15,240 square metres.

Locomotives of classes 816500 and 817000 used on suburban trains continue to be housed at La Villette. Other members of the latter class are based at La Chapelle and Achères, while members of class BB25500 are based at Montrouge (not to be confused with the former RATP depot of the same name).

In general SNCF has followed a policy of building new facilities wherever possible and today the suburban services have the benefit of being based in depots which are either up-to-date or state of the art. The result is that stock is maintained to a very high technical standard and, graffiti apart, also presents an attractive and smart external appearance.

STATIONS

As the RER lines have such a diverse history, it is difficult to give a concise account of its stations within the scope of a book of this size, since they could well merit a large and lavishly illustrated volume to themselves! There is also a considerable difference between those stations built new or altered for line A in the 1960s or for the electrification of the Sceaux line in 1937 and those which have simply been adapted when other new lines were created. One very pleasing feature of recent years, however, has been the attention paid by SNCF to the careful restoration of old station buildings, with sympathetic adaptation for use on what is essentially a mass transit system.

A close-up view of the impressive entrance to Cergy le Haut on line A.

LINE A

In the central area, between Gare de Lyon and La Défense, extremely large new stations were created. Monumental in conception, these were intended to reflect the confidence of the Fifth Republic, although in view of the growth of traffic, it is perhaps as well that the planners were inclined to think on the grand scale. These planners had few really comparable lines from which to draw experience; the nearest was the Nord-Sud line of the Berlin S-Bahn, completed in 1939, but its stations were conceived and (despite occasional interference from Hitler) executed on a much more modest scale. It is to the great credit of all those involved with the design and building of the RER stations that, faced with the task of creating stations which would be technically suited to the traffic, would reflect the prestige of the city and the state and would still convey some sense of humanity, they got it so nearly right.

From east to west, there are six such stations. Nation, designed by the architect Alain Bourbonnais, is one of the most successful. He recreated, on a grand scale, the vaulted roof of the stations of the Métro, and, rather than try to hide the scale of this vault, 228m long and 36.4m wide, he chose to emphasise it by decorating it with hundreds of tiny pieces of glass to provide a fascinating play of light. As it was expected that more eastbound than westbound passengers would have to spend time here waiting for a train, the eastbound platform is wider than that opposite.

Gare de Lyon is on five levels, the station of line A occupying the lowest, more than 25m below ground level. Much of the work was executed in reinforced concrete which, despite the use of blue and orange tiling, imparts a sombre air to the station.

Châtelet-Les-Halles may be taken to be the centre of RER operations on the Right Bank, if not in fact the centre of the whole system. Again its platforms are located at the lowest level and are situated in an enormous hall, 325m long by 79.35m wide. This houses, in all, seven tracks serving eight platform faces. Four tracks are used by trains of lines A and B, two by through trains of line D and one by terminating trains of line D. The platforms are themselves large, being 225m long by 16.72m wide. The general design of the station and the

A view of Auber station taken about 1989. The television screens were removed soon afterwards, as they had proved to be an unsuccessful form of advertising and publicity. *Brian Hardy*

The eastbound platform of line A at Nation is especially wide because it is heavily used by passengers for both eastern branches of the line. *Brian Patton*

materials used are again rather severe, in some places perhaps even brutal and, especially when few passengers are around, present an unwelcoming aspect to the traveller. The station area incorporates a large number of boutiques and food stalls, which certainly give it a more human aspect when they are open, but they tend to close after the evening peak and hide their windows behind steel shutters.

Auber is perhaps the most exciting of the central area stations and certainly presents a more attractive face to the public. It was designed by Wogenscky, a disciple of Le Corbusier, and has a blue colour scheme. In the mezzanine, the lighting scheme is of considerable interest, with light being directed from circular columns – which also cater for ventilation and transmission of sound – towards the vault. There is sufficient space in this area for events such as concerts to be held.

The interior décor of Charles de Gaulle-Étoile was designed by Pierre Dufau, who took as his inspiration cities of the far east. To create the effect of a Chinese street scene, he suspended large, illuminated publicity hoardings above the tracks, at the edge of the platforms. These both form a bridge between the brightly lit trains and the more sombre platforms and also provide a cover for lighting and ventilation cables. In recognition of its location next to one of the city's most important monuments, the seats on the platforms are of marble.

What is now Grande Arche de la Défense station is, in keeping with the buildings around it, executed in reinforced concrete. This is lightened by numerous shops and cafés on either side of the entrance hall. This was reconstructed during 1999 and 2000. A new station, Val d'Europe, was under construction between Bussy-Saint Georges and Marne la Vallée-Chessy at the end of 2000.

A station which was opened at a later stage was Bussy – Saint-Georges between Torcy and Marne-la-Vallée. It is part covered and part open to the light and until 1997 had the only escalator on either the Métro or RER with glass balustrades. *Brian Hardy*

Many of the stations on the Vincennes line were rebuilt in connexion with the transfer to RATP control and there were also many new stations. While they all share the design features of the contemporary Métro with regard to platform furniture, signage etc, they also have a refreshing dissimilarity one from another. However, all were designed in line with two basic principles – ease of interchange with local bus services and harmonisation with the suburban environment. Most are in the open and many are elevated above the surrounding land. One such, and one of the most interesting, is Lognes, situated over a small lake whose waters reflect the white concrete of the station buildings. Val-de-Fontenay is of somewhat similar design, with panels of dark glass reflecting the surroundings and a general outline chosen to harmonise with the blocks of flats nearby, while still distinguishing the station from these. However, all stations on the eastern section of line A are of interest. For those who hanker for the old days, a visit to the former station of Reuilly, on the closed section leading into Bastille, is well worth while; although no longer in railway use, the station building has been beautifully restored to its former condition and forms a pleasant link with the old Vincennes line.

Rather less work was undertaken on the Saint-Germain line, but the station at Rueil was completely rebuilt, while the terminus was replaced by a new underground station, situated to the north of the former one. While this did allow restoration of the classical formation of the park, it was unfortunate that the little circular entrance building was also demolished, despite the link it provided with the original Saint-Germain company.

Above A view of line A at Grande Arche de La Défense. *Capital Transport*

Right Opened for Eurodisney in 1992, this glasshouse style station is at the eastern end of line A, Marne la Vallée-Chessy. *RATP*

LINE B

The main features of architectural interest on line B are the stations of the former Sceaux line. Existing stations on the northern section were not rebuilt, though some are fine examples of typical architecture of the Nord company. Its most favoured design for suburban stations was of three linked pavilions, as typified by stations such as Drancy. The new station of Stade de France – Saint-Denis, already mentioned, is an excellent example of modern architecture linked to the large spaces needed to accommodate and keep moving a large crowd.

The tiled name at Fontenay-aux-Roses. *Brian Hardy*

The station building at Saint-Rémy-Lès-Chevreuse, basically unchanged from the 1890s, is a good example of the design used by the PO company for more important stations on its secondary lines. *Brian Hardy*

Unfortunately little that is good can be said about the underground station for lines B and D at Gare du Nord. It is lacking in either the grandeur of the stations of line A or the airiness and good design of those of line E. A dark colour scheme of black and orange has not been significantly brightened by new lighting. Saint-Michel, being basically a larger version of a London tube station, provided little scope for interesting design. A memorial in a cross-passage commemorates passengers killed by a terrorist bomb in this station in 1995.

But on the southern section, there is much to interest the visitor. Port-Royal is little changed since it first opened on 1 April 1895 and the station building, which, unusually, is located above the tracks, sports an attractive canopy of Art Nouveau style, pre-dating its use on the Métro by several years. The station once served a nearby maternity hospital and the drinking fountain at which mothers-to-be could slake their thirst still stands on platform 2.

Even more interesting is the station of Denfert-Rochereau which, although deprived of one of its curved wings when the line was extended to Luxembourg, still forms a charming link with Arnoux's line and is now the oldest original station in Paris, albeit somewhat altered. Designed by the engineer Dulong in 1846, the outline of the building still traces the course and dimensions of the terminal loop conceived by Arnoux. This layout had the advantage that it was not necessary to detach a locomotive from a train before that could leave for another journey and it thus reduced considerably the amount of shunting required, a manoeuvre which occupied much time at termini in those days. At this station and at Luxembourg are still to be seen monograms of the Paris/Orléans company, with its initials entwined in classic Art Nouveau fashion.

South of Denfert, some stations were rebuilt or considerably altered when the line was electrified. Platforms were raised to full height and full length canopies were fitted to many stations; these are in a restrained Art Deco style and give a certain visual harmony to the line. The stations of Cité Universitaire (formerly Sceaux-Ceinture) and Massy-Palaiseau were completely rebuilt, in each case with fine buildings, the latter designed by Louis Brachat. Unfortunately in the latter case, this is located some way from the platforms of line B, access to which is by a long footbridge. This layout was adopted to allow space for the tracks of a planned new main line to Chartres via Gallardan, which in the event was not built. However, for the enthusiast at least, the excellent view afforded over the entire complex is compensation for the long walk over this bridge. It also links line B to the platforms of line C and thus to the TGV station. The now-disused platforms at La Place, formerly used by short-working trains, are an excellent example of station architecture of the 1930s. In the outer suburbs many of the original buildings remain in use, that at Robinson having been skilfully blended with an Art Deco clock tower.

To commemorate the centenary of the Métro, several stations were redecorated with particular themes and Luxembourg was included in this scheme. The theme is ecology and nine display panels convey various topics within this field. A news sheet was also issued to passengers.

LINE C

Little work was undertaken at suburban stations when line C was created and the two central area stations are of little interest, though of course the former hotel and terminal building at Quai d'Orsay is worth more than a glance. But at rail level both this station and Saint-Michel are dark and uninspiring, although the enthusiast may pause to notice the riveted pillars, a link with the original station at Orsay. Invalides is distinctly brighter. The little station building at Javel, also designed by Litsch for use at Alma during the 1889 exhibition and moved to its present site in 1895, has been restored to original condition in recent years.

For suburban and country stations, the PO company favoured a simple design of a two-storey building with an attic and rather pretty dormers and many of these can still be seen. On the western section, many of the stations are plain, reflecting the impecunious nature of the Ouest/Etat administrations, but those on the line from Invalides are better and show much fine detail. Meudon – Val-Fleury is probably the best example. Versailles Chantiers was completely rebuilt in the early 1930s, along with its signal cabin, and both the interior and exterior of the main building show an interesting and unusual form of Art Deco styling. Other stations on the line from Montparnasse were rebuilt at the same time and in the same general style, with much use of reinforced concrete. Vanves-Malakoff, Clamart and Bellevue are all good examples of this.

For the VMI portion of line C, a good deal of conservation work was undertaken on station buildings with pleasing results, although at platform level, the underground stations are gloomy.

In complete contrast to vast stations such as Auber, the station building and crossing-keeper's house at Vauboyen, on the line from Versailles CH to Massy-Palaiseau, could be located on any rural line in France. It is typical of those built for the Grande Ceinture and, save for the television aerial, is still in virtually original condition, as seen in March 1997. *Brian Patton*

LINE D

Apart from the stations on the new link at Evry, there is little to note on the southern section. Although the PLM was a wealthy company, it did not spend much on its suburban stations, which are generally plain with a single small building. The new underground station at Gare de Lyon, although better than that at Nord, is undistinguished. Stations on the northern section have already been mentioned under line B.

The line D platforms at Châtelet les Halles where there is interchange with lines A and B. *Capital Transport*

The recently completed station at Stade de France St Denis. *Brian Perren*

LINE E

In every respect, there could not be a greater contrast between the stations provided in the central area for lines B and D and those for line E.

Magenta is located between Gare du Nord and Gare de l'Est, although at present access to the latter is only by a detour through local streets. Underground access will not be provided until the station is rebuilt for the opening of the TGV-Est in, probably, 2006. However, there is now convenient interchange with lines B and D and with several lines of the urban Métro, the flow of passengers in each direction being carefully kept apart.

The main hall of this station is lit largely by natural light, which enters through a vast window in the roof and provides a sense of airiness not previously encountered in an RER underground station. For the first time in a modern station much use has been made of wood (fire-resistant, of course) and this adds an extra dimension of warmth to the concourse. Access to trains is by both escalator and staircase to a mezzanine level, thence by pairs of escalators to the platforms. Those escalators which lead from the main concourse have their mechanism enclosed by glass only, a feature which is of both interest in itself and also increases the impression of lightness and space. The walls of the corridors which lead to the lower flights of escalators are rendered in concrete which has been frozen to give the appearance of marble and also has excellent reflecting qualities.

Magenta has four platforms and provides interchange with the main line station of Gare du Nord, lines B and D and Métro lines 4, 5 and (at La Chapelle) 2. A more dubious and less convenient interchange is possible with Gare de l'Est at street level. A ten car train of MI2N stock is seen in one of the single tunnel side platforms. *Brian Hardy*

A five car train of SNCF MI2N stock awaits departure from the present terminus of line E at Haussmann – Saint-Lazare. This station too comprises four spacious platforms on two separate islands. *Brian Hardy*

There are many escalators at both Magenta and Haussmann – Saint-Lazare. At the latter there are in all 140 in the entire station complex and some of those serving line E have uplighters, as seen here. This particular pair also has a mid-way horizontal level, which is just visible. *Brian Hardy*

Platform surfaces are of stone with a marble finish and a plinth running along the walls supports at intervals wooden seats.

Where artificial lighting is used, the general scheme is one of light green in corridors, to indicate movement, and of red on platforms, where passengers require a more restful ambience, while blue indicates interchange facilities. The main lighting comes from lamps with large glass shades, suspended from the ceiling and appearing to be flying through the air. In passages, additional lighting is provided by upright tulip shaped fittings, rather reminiscent of those once used on LT escalators, while above platform seats, reading lights are set in to the walls in individual points. This light comes from fibre optics rather than traditional bulbs, and should therefore be theft-proof.

For the first time, natural light has been allowed to penetrate a central area station of the RER. A large skylight allows plenty of daylight to illuminate the upper concourse at Magenta. *Brian Patton*

The visibility of escalator mechanism, as seen here at Haussman, is both interesting in itself and should also assist fire prevention. *Brian Patton*

One of the upper passages at Haussmann – Saint-Lazare, rendered in concrete into which fibre inserts have been placed to reduce noise levels. *Brian Patton*

Stations have been divided into 'pôles' or separate access areas and the direction signs reflect this concept. At Magenta, these are the 'Pôle Alsace' from which there is access to Gare du Nord and lines 4 and 5 of the Métro, and the 'Pôle Daint-Denis', which had direct access to lines B and D. Under these general headings, further details are given of exits and interchange. It is hoped that this will assist passengers to locate themselves easily and first indications in the autumn of 1999 suggested that the system was already working well.

In both stations, the layout at platform level is of two tracks with side platforms covered by a single vault and single tracks and platforms in individual side tunnels.

Haussmann – Saint-Lazare shares the above design features but in layout has been adapted to the different requirements of the site. It has two concourses, that of Haussmann being also lit by natural light through a window in the roof. There are more exits than at Magenta, since many more passengers will leave the station here, and most of these are located in existing or new buildings. As this is a main shopping area, there is direct access to the department store of Galeries Lafayette and another, in a new building which also houses an SNCF ticket office, near Au Printemps. The Haussmann concourse also has some shops and provides room for much technical equipment. The platform area which, as at Magenta, incorporates four roads, is of vast proportions, having a central vault of 21m. The platforms themselves are 225m long and 58m wide, the height above them being 13.5m

The 'Pôle Saint-Lazare' is concerned more with interchange with lines 3, 12, 13 and (in future) 14 of the Métro and, given the likely heavy flow of passengers and the limitations of the site (line 12 is almost directly above it) it was decided to lay out this area on two levels. Again there is complete separation of passengers entering from those leaving. As the 'Pôle Haussman' connects with Havre-Caumartin station and thus with lines 3 and 9, and as this station in turn is connected to Auber (line A) and Opéra (lines 3, 7 and 8), a vast underground interchange has been created, by which it is possible – given a ticket – to walk entirely underground from Opéra to Saint-Lazare.

Particular attention has been given to acoustics and the reduction of echoes. In the platform areas, noise reduction has been effected by cushions of concrete mousse placed in the vault and by rubber inserts in the track mountings, while in corridors the same effect is obtained by perforated wood (Magenta) and fibre inserts in concrete at Haussmann. All surfaces have been treated with an anti-graffiti solution.

The overall impression is one of user-friendliness. The stations are spacious and light, without having the sometimes overwhelming grandeur of those on line A and they are vastly more welcoming than those on lines B and D. The only possible drawback, from the operator's angle, is that they show up all too clearly the defects of these earlier stations! Many of the suburban stations were rebuilt in the 1930s when the Est company carried out a good deal of modernisation in the area and today show few features of special interest. In all cases, platforms have been raised and additional canopies provided. New signage complements that in the central area stations and passenger reaction to these improvements has been favourable, despite their relatively modest scale.

A platform view at Magenta, showing the sound-deadening material used on the ceiling and the sound baffles between the tracks and under the platform edges. The blue lamp shade indicates the exit to interchange facilities. *Brian Hardy*

Line E is the first suburban line on which facilities for passengers with special needs have been provided. Certain ticket windows have a low counter to make them accessible to passengers in wheelchairs, although not all welcome this kind of segregation and would prefer a common design accessible to all. Lifts have large windows and have been fitted with signs in braille and enlarged print, while platforms have strips allowing passengers using guide canes to find the route to the train doors independently. Similar lifts are now appearing in stations on other lines.

The architect responsible for the stations of line E is Roland Legrand.

Although much grander in size even when compared to the stations on the Jubilee Line extension in London, there is often a similarity of finish at stations. At Haussmann – Saint-Lazare, walls are finished in rough concrete or smooth concrete, the latter having massive concrete tubular beams, akin to Westminster station in London. *Brian Hardy*

SIGNALLING

Signalling on the RER network is based on SNC practice, regardless of the ownership of the various lines.

The normal form of signalling in Ile-de-France is three aspect colour light, known as BAL, 'block automatique lumineux' (automatic colour light block signal). This consists of the same colours as used on railways in Britain, but double yellows are not used in France. Signal masts also carry the number of the signal and may also display an indication F in conjunction with a red or yellow aspect; this indicates to a driver that he may proceed on sight, observing the normal rules for this. An automatic control system also repeats the signals on the chrono-tachograph in the driving cab and a train stop will come into action should a driver fail to observe a yellow signal or stop at a red one.

This system has been installed as lines have been modernised and converted for RER operation and now covers virtually the entire Region.

However, the extremely heavy traffic experienced on line A in the 1980s led to the development of a system particularly geared to the needs of its central section. This is know as SACEM – Système d'Aide à Conduite, à l'Exploitation et à la Maintenance (System to help with driving, running the service and maintenance). It was developed by a group of French manufacturers from the late 1970s onwards. This study group worked with four aims in mind – any new system should allow continual control of the speed of a train, it should be capable of use in the driving cabs of existing stock, it should be compatible with the ATO system described above and it should reduce maintenance costs. The result was SACEM, first tried in 1982 on the section of line A from Torcy to Noisiel. Following the success of that trial, it was brought into operation on the central section from Nanterre to Fontenay between July 1985 and May 1989. It has allowed the reduction of headway on this section to two minutes, thus providing a capacity, with single-deck stock, of over 50,000 passengers per direction per hour.

A view of signalling at La Varenne – Chennevières ; the departing train is running empty to Boissy depot.
Brian Hardy

The system overrides the normal signals, which are in fact switched off when it is in operation. Its use is shown by a trackside signal of a white X on a black ground. On a display panel in the cab, there is a permanent indication of the occupation of the track ahead. With this information and a knowledge of the braking parameters of the rolling stock, the system can calculate the speed at which a driver can safely drive. Should (s)he fail to observe the instructions given by the system, an emergency stop will be made by it. This allows a reduction in the length of block sections and a theoretical headway of a train every minute; given station stops, this in practice translates to a train every two minutes.

SACEM is also able to diagnose faults in signalling and this has appreciably reduced the time which has to be spent in maintenance, this in turn leading to improved reliability.

To obtain maximum benefit from SACEM, it was essential that station dwell times should not exceed 50 seconds and RATP therefore adopted the Japanese practice of having teams of platform staff whose duty it is to ensure that this is maintained. After 40 seconds have elapsed, an audible signal sounds and these staff then first ask, then physically prevent passengers from continuing to board. Although they do not resort to pushing passengers into trains, these measures have helped to maintain the closest headway on any urban rail line anywhere and to keep line A trains moving.

However, despite SACEM, numbers were still in excess of the capacity of the line, sometimes reaching a figure of 63,000 passengers per hour in the peak, and it was clear that only by the building of new lines would permanent relief be afforded to line A.

The white X on the indication denotes that SACEM is in operation at Grande Arche de La Défense.
Brian Hardy

Signalling and cctv monitors for one-person operation at the north end of Châtelet station.
Brian Hardy

CONTROL

Only lines A and B have dedicated control centres, those on other lines being shared with other services.

On the former, the Poste de Commande et Controle (PCC) is located at Vincennes and is similar to those which supervise the urban Métro. A line diagram shows the position of every train, the aspect of every signal and the condition of the distribution system of current. This information is conveyed to the PCC by trackside equipment which works in conjunction with on-board transmitters. Controllers are in radio touch with drivers and can also control the supply of current. Announcements can be made over a public address system to stations on the line and platform indicators are remotely controlled by computer. The control centre for line B is situated at Denfort-Rochereau.

However, in conjunction with the building of line E, a new signalling and control centre was created with responsibility for the tunnel section and also the surface lines as far as Val-de-Fontenay and Raincy. This post is actually located in an otherwise unremarkable building in an ordinary Paris street. It was therefore no easy task to fit in to this building a control panel with a total length of twenty metres, but the architects succeeded in doing so and ensuring at the same time that the displays would be legible from any part of the control room.

The new system is based closely on information technology. For operational purposes, the area has been divided into 23 zones, under the direction of six controllers, one of whom has particular responsibility for line E. These work under supervision of a 'chef de circulation' (traffic manager) who has overall responsibility for both line E and the other lines in the area concerned. Passenger information systems, mentioned elsewhere, are controlled from this centre, which came into operation in 1998.

The development of this new centre has no doubt contributed to the relatively smooth inauguration of line E, since it has allowed other facilities in the area to be adapted to the increased pace of operation required by an RER line.

FARES AND TICKETS

Information in this section covers both the Métro and the RER/SNCF services.

The fare system on the urban Métro has always been relatively simple. From the beginning a flat fare was used and the original fare of 15 centimes second class remained in force until 1919.

Thereafter successive increases took it to 45 francs by 1958. First class fares were always approximately 50% higher. Return tickets which cost about 25% more than a single journey were available in second class until 1938. Books of single tickets, known as 'carnets' have always been available but did not carry any discount until 1949. Since then the discount has been steadily increased and is now about 40%. In practice most passengers who do not use one or other of the season tickets buy a carnet and very few travel on ordinary single tickets. There were always 'social' fares for such groups as war-disabled and large families and under the Vichy government 12-journey weekly tickets were introduced, which are still available, though now much less used.

First class fares were abolished under President Mitterand in August 1991. While they did not bring much extra comfort, they did bring some welcome extra space in the rush hour! They were still available on the RER until September 1999.

Until 1951 ordinary single tickets carried the name of the issuing station and first class tickets carried this until they were withdrawn. Tickets were colour coded, the first colours used being pink, grey and green for first class, second class and returns respectively. Colours were changed from time to time and the Nord-Sud company used different colours, sometimes in combination with distinguishing marks such as a blue band. At certain times, the reverse of tickets was used for advertisements or publicity, but since 1973 the reverse has had a brown magnetic strip for use in automatic barriers. From 1951 second class tickets were yellow and from 1973 all tickets were yellow until 1992, when they were changed to jade green, following the introduction of new house colours by RATP. From 1968 the same tickets were used on the rail, bus and (latterly) tram services.

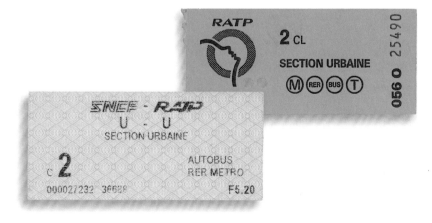

The fare system on suburban railways was always based on traditional rail practice, using Edmonson card tickets. A complete history would fill a book of its own – suffice it to say here that special fares for such services were introduced slowly over the years, usually with a strong rearguard action from the railway companies, who feared for their profitability. Concessions were of course standardised after the creation of SNCF in 1938.

The opening of the first portion of line A in 1969 saw the first use of automatic ticket checking in the Paris area, together with a zone fare system which was based closely on that introduced on the Sceaux line when it was transferred to CMP control in the 1930s. In most cases these fares represented a reduction for the passenger. The success of automatic ticket checking led to the introduction of a similar system on the Métro, which, after a transition period, was fully operational in October 1974. This rendered redundant the famous 'tricoteuses' (knitters) – the usually female ticket checkers who were renowned for their

ability to examine up to 30 tickets per minute while continuing with their knitting and few fare-evaders ever escaped their scrutiny, nor did anyone try to escape them by the more recent practice of jumping over barriers

However, the energy crisis which followed the increase in petrol prices in 1973 made the authorities appreciate the need for a more radical new approach to the whole matter of ticketing in the Paris area, both to make public transport more attractive and to avoid penalising passengers who had to use more than one mode of transport to complete their journey. There was also the matter of the harmonisation of the different systems of the RATP and the SNCF which would be necessary with the creation of further lines of the RER – when line C was first opened, RATP tickets were not valid on the urban section and this caused much confusion and resentment among passengers. The result of this idea was the Carte Orange, which first came into operation on 30 June 1975.

The Carte consists of an orange ticket, with photograph of the holder, to which is attached a coupon for the area and period of validity. At first these coupons were monthly only, but later both weekly and annual coupons have been available, the latter being based on 10.5 times the monthly rate. The Paris area was divided for this purpose into five concentric zones, the carte being sold for a minimum of two adjacent zones. It is valid on all RATP bus, tram and rail services, all RER services, all other SNCF suburban service and the bus services operated in the suburbs by private operators.

To say that the Carte Orange was a success would be a grave understatement. It was received with quite-unforeseen enthusiasm by the public and is now used by almost half of all travellers in the area. Bus services were the main beneficiaries but all forms of transport recorded an increase in passenger numbers. The principle was later copied by other cities and was the direct inspiration for the London Travelcard. The success of the Carte Orange has shown beyond any doubt that the possibility of making a journey which, from the ticketing angle, is seamless will encourage passenger numbers.

The weekly version, at first called Carte Jaune, was made available from 1 November 1982. The annual Carte Intégrale followed later.

On 1 January 1991 the scope of the Carte Orange was extended to cover the entire region of Ile-de-France, which was divided into eight zones, to the benefit of users of outer-suburban services. At the same time, the Carte itself was redesigned and in size now resembles a credit card. As a protection against forgery, it is now sealed in a plastic cover once it has been completed by the user. An extensive publicity campaign, under the theme of 'uniting', was launched to promote the new Carte Orange and again it recorded a great success, the number of passengers on suburban lines increasing by almost 4% within a year.

TICKETS FOR THE VISITOR

Mobilis is a one-day ticket available in various combinations of zones but not to the airports of Roissy or Orly. Strictly speaking it is intended only for inhabitants of Ile-de-France, and the visitor from abroad or the provinces should buy a Paris Visite ticket, which is available for zones 1–3, 1–5 and 1–8. This of course includes the airports, where the ticket may be bought, and also Euro-Disney. The ticket may be bought for one, three or five days and confers the advantage of a reduction on the entry charge to 15 tourist sites in the region. A photograph is not required, though a coupon is issued with the ticket and the two are only valid together; the number of a passport or identity card should be inscribed on the coupon. Users should note that the ticket should NOT be inserted into cancellers on board buses and trams. Visitors staying for longer than five days should buy a weekly Carte Orange (coupon hebdomadaire) but this of course requires a photograph. The ticket's validity is from Monday to Sunday and again it should not be cancelled on buses or trams. These details are correct as of July 2000 but could be changed at a later date.

BIBLIOGRAPHY

This bibliography covers sources used in preparation of both the present work and the companion volume on the urban Métro by Brian Hardy.

Encyclopédie Générale des Transports, fascicules 13, 14, 15. Éditions de l'Ormet, Valignat, 1995

Le Patrimoine de la RATP. L J de Niewmierzycki (ed.) *et al*. Éditions Flohic, Paris, 1996

Notre Métro. Jean Robert. 2nd edition, Paris, 1983.

Le Métro de Paris. Abindi et D Lefeuvre. Éditions Ouest-France, 1990

Du Madeleine-Bastille à Météor, Histoire des Transports Parisiens. Éditions Martelle, Amiens, 1992

Métro Mémoire. Vincent Lautié, ed. RATP et Centre régionale Documentation pédagogique de l'acadèmie de Créteil, Créteil, 1991

Le Métro de Chez Nous. J-C Demory. Éditions MDM, Boulogne, 1997

Vincennes-Maillot, la construction de la Ligne 1. A Tartié *et al*. Bibliothèque de la Ville de Paris, Paris, 1998

Fulgence Bienvenüe et la Construction du Métroploitian de Paris. C Berton et A Ossadzow avec C Filloles. Presses de l'École Nationale de Ponts et Chaussées, Paris, 1998

Il était une Fois le Métro. Connassaince du Rail, special number, no. 63, 1986

Naissance d'un Métro (line 14). La Vie du Rail, Paris, 1998

Les Transports en Région Parisienne. P Merlin. Études de la Documentation Francaise, Paris, 1997

Paris Ferroviaire. C Lamming. Éditions Parisgramme, Paris, 1999

La Petite Ceinture de Paris. Various authors. Éditions de l'Ormet, Valignat, 1991

La Ligne C du RER. A Jacquot et P Laedorich. Éditions de l'Ormet, Valignat, 1989

La Lligne de Sceaux. Gaston Jacob. La Vie du Rail, Paris, 1987

Revue Générale des Chemins de Fer, no 8/9 (Eole, line E). Paris, 1996

Éole, un Voyage à travers l'Histoire. SNCF et ClioMédia, Paris, 1992

Les Trains de Banlieue, tomes 1 et 2. B Carrière. La Vie du Rail, Paris, 1998 & 1999

L'An 2001 en Ile-de-France. La Vie du Rail, Paris, 1991

Les Transports en Ile-de-France 1995–2010. La Vie du Rail, Paris, 1995

French Railways, 3rd edition. B Garvin, D Haydock and P Fox, Platform 5, Sheffield, 1999

Les Expositions Universelles et les Transports. J Robert (ed.), Musée des Transports Urbains, Paris – Saint-Mandé, 1989.

PERIODICALS

La Vie du Rail
Rail Passion
Connaissance du Rail
Chemins de Fer
Der Stadtverkehr
Modern Railways
Today's Railways

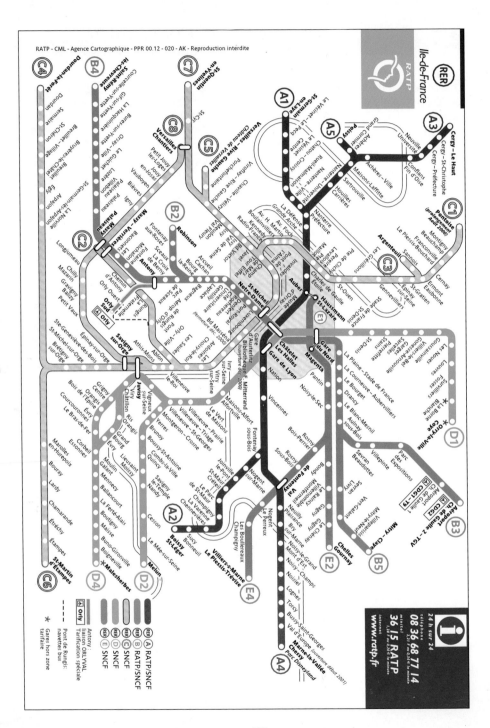